Praise for *"How Much Did You Pay For Her?"*

"How Much Did You Pay for Her?" is a much-needed book! Christine Rhyner brings all the hurtful remarks about adoptees and their families into the light. This will be a great tool for parents who are training their kids how to respond to cruel remarks, as well as a tool for clinicians to train families on how to be street smart. (By the way, I cost 57 cents.)

Sherrie Eldridge
author of *Twenty Things Adopted Kids Wish Their Adoptive Parents Knew,*
20 Things Adoptive Parents Need to Succeed

The journey of adoption is full of unique challenges, not the least of which are the comments, often well-meaning, of family, friends and even strangers. Christine Rhyner shares her very helpful perspective as an adoptive parent who has experienced these painful comments and invites the reader to apply the biblical principles of grace, forgiveness and peacemaking rather than resentment and bitterness.

Any person who has gone through infertility and has walked the path of adoption will find in Ms. Rhyner's work both an author who keenly understands the common anguish and hurts that come with the wounding comments of family and friends, as well as useful insights and applications for navigating these from the perspective of biblical principles. Thank you, Christine, for not only acknowledging the offense and pain caused by others, often unknowingly, but leading the reader down the vital path of grace and forgiveness that is often sorely missing in adoption literature.

Jeffrey L. Nitz, LCSW
Vice President of Adoption and Family Services
Bethany Christian Services

Rhyner's book is a positive paradox of moderation and extremes. Averse to legalism, she is a welcome voice of moderation when it comes to issues of assisted reproductive technology, name-it-and-claim-it theology, and the "just rely on God, not on science" mentality. She brings to her adoption story a balanced view of spiritual warfare, and a modest view of each person's role in the life of adopted children (we cannot save the world). On the other hand, Rhyner is extreme in her dispensation of grace and forgiveness. She is unrelenting in her desire to understand, rather than react to, the potentially hurtful comments that adoptive parents inevitably hear. Although there is nothing selfish about Rhyner's quest to extend grace to those around her, the journey is largely about the self. For example, she says, "It humbles me to consider the possibility that the adoption of my children has far more to do with God's plan for their lives than with my desire to have given birth to them." She sees her adoption as a tool through which God developed character traits within her. We would all do well to examine our own histories to see how God used them as a tool for fashioning us into His image.

Daniel Nehrbass, Ph.D.
President of Nightlight Christian Adoptions,
Home of the Snowflake® Embryo Adoption program

For adoptive parents (especially those who have adopted internationally), Christine Rhyner's *"How Much Did You Pay For Her?"* will come as a welcome source of wisdom and hope for dealing with all the comments, assumptions, and off-base attitudes that adoptive parents must often face. Filled with personal examples, Biblical wisdom, and insights based on real experience, Rhyner leads readers on a journey through various hurts and how to heal and offer forgiveness through each one. I recommend *"How Much Did You Pay for Her?"* as a valuable resource for those facing the unique challenges and joys of adoption.

Marlo Schalesky
author of *Empty Womb, Aching Heart: Hope and Help for Those Struggling*
with Infertility

Christine's book is an excellent and unique resource for anyone that has ever thought about adoption – or ever been a part of a conversation that included the topic of adoption. The questions and topics deal with important and sensitive information in a practical, encouraging and biblical way that can be "conversation starters" by families, individuals and/or study groups. This book will definitely open your eyes to many different aspects of adoption that many people have never considered. I highly recommend this as a resource for anyone involved in the ministry of adoption, foster care and orphan care.

Kevin Burdette
"Hope for 100" Adoption Ministry Coordinator and Minister of Adult Impact
Green Acres Baptist Church, Tyler, TX

I love that Christine has wonderfully put into words many of the thoughts and feelings that we as adoptive parents have shared. Every successful adoption is truly a miracle and even the most well-meaning of our family members ask questions with love, but may minimize the effort and faith that adoption takes. Christine's strong faith grounds her answers, her family, and ultimately the path that led her to adoption. Excellent book for all families created by adoption.

Mardie Caldwell
is Founder and CEO of Lifetime Adoption Center
with offices in California and Florida

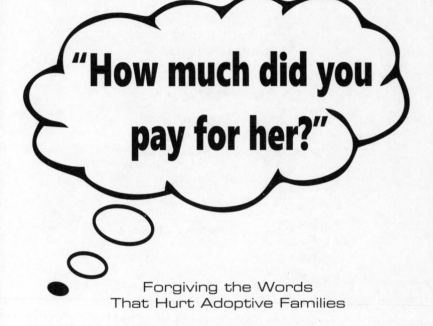

"How much did you pay for her?"

Forgiving the Words
That Hurt Adoptive Families

Christine Rhyner

CLC PUBLICATIONS

Fort Washington, PA 19034

"How Much Did You Pay for Her?"

Published by CLC Publications

U.S.A.
P.O. Box 1449, Fort Washington, PA 19034

UNITED KINGDOM
CLC International (UK)
51 The Dean. Alresford, Hampshire, SO24 9BJ

© 2014 by Christine Rhyner

ALL RIGHTS RESERVED. Published 2014

Printed in the United States of America

ISBN-13 (Trade paper): 978-1-61958-168-5
ISBN-13 (E-book): 978-1-61958-169-2

Contents

Introduction: How Do I Respond to Words that Hurt?....................... 7

PART 1: THE PATH TO ADOPTION

Chapter 1:   It's Not Fair! 15
Chapter 2:   We Here Just Trust God for Pregnancies...................27
Chapter 3:   You Just Don't Have Enough Faith! 39
Chapter 4:   Now You'll Get Pregnant! 49
Chapter 5:   You Adopted, So You Can't Have Kids, Right?..........59
Chapter 6:   Who Could Just Throw Away Her Kid Like That?....67

PART 2: NOT IN FRONT OF THE KIDS!

Chapter 7:   Do You Have Any of Your Own Children? 79
Chapter 8:   Do They Know They're Adopted? 89
Chapter 9:   Are They, You Know, Normal?..................................97
Chapter 10:   Do They Know Their Families?...............................107
Chapter 11:   How Much Did You Pay for Her?...........................117
Chapter 12:   You're So Lucky! 127

PART 3: TRANSRACIAL FAMILY AND ETHNIC OFFENSES

Chapter 13:   Why's He Sweating? You'd Think He'd Be
                        Used to the Heat! 139
Chapter 14:   She's Such a Little China Doll! 147
Chapter 15:   Hello, Little Glasshoppa! 157
Chapter 16:   Bow, Sweetie...167
Chapter 17:   He Must Be Smart and Electronically Savvy 177

PART 4: DON'T SAY IT TO THE PARENTS

Chapter 18: You're Such Good People for Adopting! 189
Chapter 19: If You Don't Expose Them to Their Cultures,
             You'll Deny Them Their Heritage 199
Chapter 20: Are You Her Real Mother? 209
Chapter 21: Just Like One of the Family 217
  Appendix: Recommended Resources 225
             Notes 227

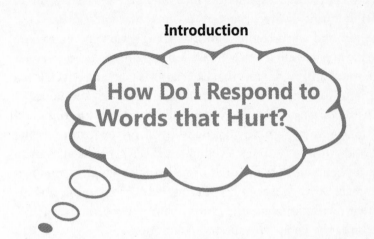

How Do I Respond to Words that Hurt?

I first faced the frightening prospect of infertility as a twenty-year-old college student diagnosed with endometriosis. The surgeon's crushing announcement to me that day was the first in a long string of hurtful and damaging words that I was to hear in the years to come. Stung with disappointment and with a sense of my own failures, I floundered through my twenties, handling my self-hatred with self-abuse.

I found Christ at the age of thirty, but this was only the beginning of learning to forgive those who had hurt me—and of extending grace to myself. Finally married to a wonderful man in my mid-thirties and desperate to start a family, I endured letdown after letdown as our hopes of conceiving a child were dashed, one blow at a time.

My husband and I were eventually led to international adoption, an arduous experience in itself, but one through which I gained a tremendous measure of healing and joy. Our son, from Vietnam, and our daughter, from China, are treasured gifts from God. Still, even after receiving the desire of my heart, I have continued over the years to field misguided comments and questions from others.

To these I have learned, and am learning, to respond with grace.

Any couple that experiences infertility and then takes on an adoption journey will be exposed to words that hurt. From "Gee, if you just had a little more faith that you'd get pregnant" to "Are those kids really yours?" we who walk this path are subject to a lot of questions and comments that can cause us pain and anger. Ours is a unique journey filled with sorrow and loss, faith and hope.

In the dozens of books I've read about others' infertility and adoption journeys, I have glimpsed bits of my own story. Being able to identify with others, even in small ways, has been to me a soothing balm and has at times provided me a laugh at my own insecurities or fears. But in my reading I also came to the conclusion that there existed no one source that wove together the many threads that make up the tapestry of adoption.

It would have been of incalculable benefit to me and my loved ones if we'd had an informative, understanding source that covered the time from, say, well before a couple boards a plane to a foreign country to adopt a baby to the time their adopted child is several years old. A book such as this, had it included the strongest and brightest threads running through it not just of faith but also of forgiveness, would have been as a work of art to me. Faith is a prerequisite for adopting a child, in particular for adopting internationally. We need faith that our adoption agency will pull everything together to make things happen. Faith that another country's government and officials will legitimately do their part. Faith that the child whose picture or video we have received is meant to be ours. Faith that the pilot who is flying our child to his or her new home country won't crash the plane.

Some of the authors whose adoption stories I read spoke of faith in God, others of faith in themselves or in destiny. But none seemed to make mention of another essential ingredient prerequisite to adoption: forgiveness. The sources on adoption that I read simply did not tell me that I had to forgive anyone for anything, why I had to forgive them or how to accomplish this.

But just think for a moment about the enormous need for mastering the art of forgiving—and of forgiving over and over—within the realm of adoption.

Adoptive parents quite often need to make peace with themselves, and sometimes with God, for damaged or broken reproductive systems that refuse to create life or for the loss of life through miscarriage or stillbirth.

Sometimes we must forgive those who hurt us before we adopted—those who judged us for not becoming pregnant or for seeming to rub their pregnant bellies in our faces while we ached and longed for a baby to love. Maybe people asked us why we would go way over there—to China or the Ukraine or India—for a child. They may have insisted that there would be something wrong with the baby we had already committed our love and lives to before we'd ever met him or her.

We need to forgive doctors who give up on patients because they are worried about their success rates. Those of us who do not meet their protocols for producing babies prove unlikely candidates for fulfilling their success rates, and they may turn us away. They can tell us to consider adoption, but they can't prepare us for how our empty wombs will affect us when we walk out their doors for the last time.

Adopted children, even at quite early ages, can begin to hold resentments against the birth parents who gave them up for reasons their young minds struggle to understand. I realized this when my barely six-year-old daughter from China looked down into her cereal bowl one morning and out of the blue exclaimed, "My own mother didn't even want me!"

Birth parents whom we and our children may never know, but whom we probably think of from time to time, have to forgive themselves for the choices they have made. And all those involved in adoption in any way should forgive a society at large for its stereotypes, misconceptions and insensitivity directed toward them.

Some parents may have a difficult time forgiving their adoption agency if it acted unscrupulously. Though most are run with integrity and do their best to work with foreign nations, we may find ourselves at odds with them for extraordinary delays in getting our children or for the ways we are treated in other countries. This happened to my husband and me while we were in Vietnam adopting our son when our adoption facilitator practically tried to force us to take a second child against our better judgment.

The church too, while it strengthens our faith in God, can also give us more than a little practice at honing our forgiveness skills. All of us have a tendency to expect much from others who, like us, have committed to loving others with the love of Christ. We sometimes fail to accept members of Christ's body as flawed, sinful individuals, just as we are.

The truth is, it takes exceptional people to steadfastly walk with a couple through the enduring hardships of infertility and adoption. If you find a few, consider yourself greatly blessed. I know that there are wonderful churches out there that will counsel and encourage a couple that is struggling with an all-consuming desire for a baby.

Although some will feel safe enough to look to the church in the midst of infertility, not many will be prepared for certain ramifications of doing so. For instance, unanticipated scenarios such as finding ourselves at odds with our church's view of fertility interventions, with our inability to conceive or with adoption itself may play themselves out. Positions on these matters will vary from church to church. It is probable that a church will be unable to offer absolute conclusions regarding the ever-increasing medical technologies available, from artificial insemination to ovary transplants.

Once we are home and settling in with our new child or children, we sometimes find ourselves broadsided by intrusive and hurtful words about our children that we never expected. My experiences have run the gamut from complete strangers approaching me to ask the cost of my children to people asking whether or not my kids are normal to others wondering aloud if my children are really brother and sister. Even my loved ones and friends have poked fun at my kids' heritages or have silenced their own children when their kids have asked if I really am my son's and daughter's mother. On the other hand, there have been times when I have been guilty of making my own erroneous assumptions about adoption too and have had to forgive myself.

It is important for us to acknowledge and deal with hurtful words and to explore the motivations behind them. Doing so is a means of trying to understand those who have hurt us. Understanding why people say what they do is the first step toward compassion, as it allows us to glimpse another's perspective. This can lead to giving others grace—an undeserved gift of letting people off the hook for what they say—that eventually leads us to forgive them, which is this book's ultimate goal.

Forgiving others lessens the damaging effects of people's repetitive negative verbal assaults on us and on our families, and it prepares us for future difficult encounters or exchanges. It is the key to freedom, to fully ridding ourselves of another's transgression toward us or ours toward them. Forgiveness maintains and builds on relationships with those we care about. It also prepares us and our children for uncomfortable situations with people who sometimes say unexpected things in every place from the grocery store to the family dinner table.

If we can develop a better understanding of the motivations behind what sometimes seems to be a never-ending stream of questions and comments, and if we can at the same time address how these exchanges really make us feel, then with the desire to forgive in our hearts, asked for from God, we can respond positively to people and transform loss into gain. We can take back our voices and our stories. We can develop all-important skills for inevitable conflict resolution as we parent our adopted children.

It is my hope that this book will be useful to anyone whose life has been impacted by adoption. As for the family, friends, co-workers, professionals, adoption agencies, churches or any others involved with an infertile couple or adoptive parent, if you love and respect these individuals, and if you hope to avoid saying or doing anything injurious in your support of them, this book can help you too.

PART 1
The Path to Adoption

1

It's Not Fair!

I cannot forget the day, when I was twenty years old, when my surgeon walked into my hospital room, stood at the edge of my bed and announced to me, "If you want children, you'd better have them now."

Still groggy from anesthesia, I just looked at her and thought about my cheating boyfriend, my unfinished college education and my lack of maturity, and in my mind I responded to her, *You must be joking.*

But she wasn't.

She had just performed a partial bilateral oophorectomy on me, because of which half of my endometriosis-ravaged ovaries were now gone. Actually, as my surgeon put it, "We took what was no good."

I blamed myself for this turn of events. During my previous college year, I had experienced months of the most sudden and horrific pain at the onset of my menstrual cycles, pain that left me in a fetal position on my bed for days. Yet I hadn't scheduled a gynecological exam. What I had done a couple times was land in the emergency room of two different hospitals, certain that I was at death's door.

One of the two ER doctors I had seen had mentioned that I might have a case of endometriosis, but he had never explained the condition to me. He hadn't told me that endometriosis is the result of the membrane that lines the womb, which is normally shed during a menstrual cycle, not being eliminated. Nor had he let me know that my ovaries, where the membrane had been deposited and had grown like wildfire, could be at the mercy of this disease. He had urged me to see a gynecologist, however. But as a broke college student who had no medical insurance and a good case of denial, I had put such a visit off.

Now I had nobody to blame but myself. Had a doctor caught my condition early on, I may have been spared the loss of so many eggs and the resulting infertility that would later cause me to soak my pillow so many nights with a thousand tears.

But that wasn't all I blamed myself for. I had ruined a relationship with a man whom I cared a great deal for but had mistreated right into the arms of someone else. There was no chance now that we would marry after college and have babies together, and it was apparent to me that I had a lot of growing up to do before I ever got to the point of having a family. No, I didn't foresee babies in my future for quite some time, and by the time I was mature enough to mother them, I reasoned, it would be too late.

Perhaps some of the greatest hurts that we who face infertility suffer are self-directed. Unlike deciding to achieve a degree or acquire a job or reach for any other milestone in life, our decision to conceive a child may result in complete failure. And nobody tells us how this failure will hit us. No experience prepares us for how our identity will warp and morph into a version of self that can frighten and grieve us. Even if we have strong faith in God, which I developed over the years following my initial heartbreak, being confronted with infertility may bring us to a sort of spiritual crisis. We may tell ourselves that we are a failure. Or defective. Or unworthy. Or unfeminine. The list goes on.

Infertility has been, without a doubt, the biggest obstacle in my life to self-acceptance and forgiveness. Self-loathing over the belief that I was responsible for my empty womb due to my poor choices and behavior turned my inability to have a baby into a runaway train. It sped off, taking with it all the essential ingredients of a life worth living: gratitude, joy, peace, love and contentment. The anger I felt toward myself and toward God gave my infertility the fuel that propelled it ever faster toward my destruction.

You see, I wasn't just immature. I also had a drinking problem that resulted in my being in a state of arrested development emotionally, psychologically and spiritually. God, back then, was someone whom I rarely gave a thought to. And why should I have? I had been told many years earlier that I was selfish and would never have children, so apparently God had made me that way. There was nothing for me to think about but myself and the next party I could attend.

I wasted a lot of time in early years. But I finally reached out to God when I was thirty, and He reached right back and scooped me out of the pit that was my life. Yet He still had much healing to do in me before I was ready for Mr. Right. It wasn't until I was thirty-five years old that I met my wonderful husband.

I remember sitting in John's car one night. I felt it only fair to tell him that I might not ever be able to have children. He nodded his head and said, "Well, I don't feel a burning need to procreate." And he never has!

He loves me without conditions and has never once expressed disappointment that he might not become a father to a biological child. He has also always supported my attempts at becoming pregnant and offered me compassion when they failed. Because despite my medical history and my "advanced age" of over thirty-five that placed a hoped-for pregnancy in the high-risk category, I believed that God could bless us with a healthy baby.

But as the years passed and medical interventions to achieve pregnancy became more costly and physically invasive, a realization dawned in me that God just might keep the door shut on conception and childbirth for me. Oh, how I grieved for the baby that would not come! Green horns of envy for others' fertility began to poke their way through my skull. I felt disconnected and alone amidst a sea of fertile family and friends.

Wearing my heart on my sleeve made others notice my pain. And this only increased my angst. People attempted to replace my horns with hope by way of a plethora of advice and stories of pregnancy miracles. One told me, "Stand on your head for three minutes after intercourse." Another, "You should probably see a chiropractor." And one of my favorites, "My friend knows this woman who got pregnant, and she doesn't even have fallopian tubes!" I heard it all. It seemed as if everyone who crossed my grief-stricken path wanted to throw something at me to see if their advice would stick.

Sometimes well-intentioned church friends encouraged me to attend this or that healing service. Some instructed me on how to effectively pray for a child. Others decided that I needed to be delivered from a "spirit of infertility." One person suggested, "Just ask God why you're not getting pregnant, because there's probably sin in your life that He wants you to deal with."

I pursued many of these suggestions. Still no pregnancy. And soon all those enthusiastic voices silenced themselves. In the hush and emptiness of those years existed moments of being ignored that felt unbearable. Some friends and acquaintances coolly withdrew from me. In my mind I wore a scarlet letter "I" for "Infertile" stamped across my forehead.

When I was with those who loved and supported me, try as I might, I could not keep the pain to myself. It snuck out in my conversations with them. They changed the subject. One friend even forbade me to mention my infertility woes any longer when she informed me, "I'm not a counselor."

In fact, I was seeing a counselor, but still there was all this pent-up anger that rose up out of me like a storm. Frequently I lashed out at my poor husband and at God. Anger is like that. It either turns inward and becomes depression and self-hatred, or it targets those whom we dearly love and feel safest with and who love us right back despite our shortcomings.

"It's not fair!" I shouted at the Lord. "Why have you given babies to all five of my sisters but not to me? What have I done that's so awful to deserve this?" The crushing silence from Him reminded me of when my parents would ignore my childhood temper tantrums.

But as children often do with parents who deny them of their wants, I would then burst into tears and seek comfort from my heavenly Father even in the misery I felt that He was responsible for. Sorry and sad, I wanted to draw close to Him and to know that He loved me and wasn't angry with me for my juvenile behavior and bad thoughts. Still not understanding why His answer was no, the conflict within me that came from being angry with the One I most looked up to was too difficult to bear.

So the cycle continued with more self-loathing. I despised my empty womb—dark, barren, inhospitable place it turned out to be. I was defective, and that defect distorted the very essence of my femininity.

Outside my private, personal hell, life went on around me. Friends and family became pregnant and with enthusiasm shared their news with me. While glad for them, I experienced a kind of validation within me that everyone was deemed worthy of bearing a child except me. I wondered if all my Christian friends and family were, well, better Christians than I was.

When the last of my friends who had endured years of infertility finally became pregnant, my sorrow was incalculable. The one person who had remained in my life and who could understand my emptiness had been blessed too. I now stood utterly alone, barren, broken and cursed.

And when she found herself with a second pregnancy on the heels of giving birth to her first child, I wanted to scream at her when she told me, "I didn't want this to happen again so soon. I'm getting on birth control after this one."

And then came our adoption plan and our joy. Yet even that did not erase all the pain and self-condemnation nor cease the questions that I posed to God about what I had experienced. Those issues take time to heal.

What Hurts

When I first saw a gynecologist about my medical history with endometriosis and the difficulties of conceiving that go along with it, I received compassion from him—and a great story. He shared with me that his wife dealt with the same condition I did. She had undergone in vitro fertilization. He told me, "All we had was one embryo to implant. That embryo's name is now Aaron, and he is five years old."

That story was like a shot of vitamin B12 to my spirit. If Jesus could feed five thousand with a few fish and several loaves of bread, he could use just one of my eggs to create an embryo that would become a little person.

But when our fertility specialist refused to proceed with IVF with less than three eggs, I told him what our gynecologist had said. I even contacted the doctor and asked him to advocate for us. He said he would. But it didn't change things. Rules were rules, our fertility doctor told us, and no exceptions would be made.

The world of reproductive technologies is a murky and confusing place. If a couple will undergo difficult, painful procedures, invest precious time in follow-through with them and pay exorbitant fees for a chance to become biological parents, they should have a greater say in how that treatment is handled—despite how it may affect a clinic's success rates.

I believe that the desire to have children is a God-given one; unmet, it can turn into a consuming grief. It's as the thirteenth chapter of the book of Proverbs says: "Hope deferred makes the heart sick" (13:12).

In desperation, many of us infertile couples wage war against our heart sickness. As this battle begins, the troops of family, friends, fellow churchgoers, counselors and others pour in and offer their assistance.

While the support is appreciated at first, the battlefield can start to blur into a sea of combatants in which it's difficult to distinguish friend from foe. That's because a battle requires a strategic plan and a united front, with everyone in it for the long haul. Yet the combat zone can appear to be filled with scattered troops who plow ahead with their own battle plan, then mysteriously desert the field!

Great confusion flooded me during the raging war within me because of all the advice I received on how I should achieve conception. My confidence was shaken by having my faith and my sins and my choices dissected by others.

The process shredded any self-worth I'd had. I doubted my every move during the battle. Cornered and blasted by loaded barrels of hurtful words, I gave way to nursing my spiritual, emotional and physical wounds. Even so, in my battered condition I was expected to drag myself to baby showers, children's birthday parties and maternity wards to visit others' new babies. I forced myself to congratulate friends on their swollen bellies full of new life, to ask about their health and to help out new mothers.

God was the only One who had all the answers and the right direction for me to follow. At first I couldn't quite hear Him amidst the cacophony of voices that filled my head. As time wore on, however, the din faded, and I needed Him more than ever, because the troops had packed up and gone home, leaving me alone in my pain. One extreme had replaced another, and that hurt.

Grace Given

It is impossible for us to dwell in a place of self-condemnation, anger toward God and disappointment in people for long. We can't love, know that we are loved or have relationship with God or anyone else in such a state of mind.

The first step toward self-forgiveness is to give grace.

Just as someone who hurts or offends us takes "junk" from his or her heart and dumps it on us, self-condemnation is when we pull ugliness from our own hearts and cast it on ourselves. We dwell on it, bathe in it, rub it all over ourselves—and it stinks. It burns. It keeps others away from us, and it keeps us in pain. We have to accept God's provision of forgiveness to take away the hurt.

If I don't give grace to myself or to another person who hurts me—if I don't let my offenders off the hook, so to speak—then my decision to withhold forgiveness negates the core of my faith. It's tantamount to telling God that someone is unforgivable, that Christ's death on the cross and His forgiveness for the sins of all mankind throughout the ages is insufficient for the forgiveness of my sins or another's sins. Who can say that she believes in God and what His Son has done for us when in the basement of her psyche she stockpiles a ll the hurtful, harmful things that she has done to herself and that others have done to her? This only allows the root of bitterness to take hold within us.

In her book *Living Beyond Your Feelings*, Joyce Meyer asks, "What is the seed from which that root sprouts? Unforgiveness! Bitterness results from the many minor offenses committed against us that we just won't let go of." She also acknowledges that "there are sometimes major offenses committed against us. The longer we allow bitterness and resentment to grow and fester, the more of a problem they become and the harder it is to be free from them . . . the best thing to do regarding any offense, large or small, is to forgive quickly and completely."[1] Not only does holding onto bitterness grieve the Holy Spirit (see Eph. 4:30), but it contaminates us and those we come into contact with.

I choose grace for those who haven't experienced infertility, because the problem is difficult for the fertile to comprehend.

Those who marry, plan a family, conceive and bear children just might take all these things for granted as a normal course of life events. They never have to feel the anguish that many of us do over a broken body. They don't question God as to why He hasn't allowed them to become mothers to biological children.

They do not have to exhaustively explore complex issues such as fertility interventions or face the judgment of family and friends who shun them. They will never feel as if they want to sink into the floor at a baby shower. Tears do not flow from their swollen eyes while they watch mothers in the park with their babies. And they aren't horrified by the onset of each period, riding a sickening roller coaster of hope and despair each month until they find themselves ready to jump off at the crest before yet another downhill run.

But I choose grace, because I know that those who love me will never understand and that they do want to help. I need to remember that I live in a culture of doers and fixers. When I present people with a problem, they try to come up with an answer.

Some of the suggestions and pieces of advice we receive can be helpful. We should be open and should receive them when they are offered by loving, wise sources. If I suffer through years of attempting to achieve a pregnancy and then years more on an adoption journey, I need to understand that family and friends can suffer burnout in their efforts to support me throughout what seems to them an infinite emotional struggle.

It isn't the intention of most infertile couples to diminish the joy that others feel about their own babies. Yet I realize that we don't always come across as the most enthusiastic participants in people's lives. We sometimes avoid our pregnant friends. We sit way back in the room at a baby shower or leave the nursery decorating or the baby-clothes shopping to other friends. We can let others down.

Lastly, doctors deserve grace too. Many do care about their patients and want to make wise decisions in their best interests. Unfortunately, many must adhere to protocol and guidelines for specific clinics.

Handling It

We have to remember throughout our grief and in any self-blame that God's Word tells us, "There is therefore now no condemnation for those who are in Christ Jesus" (Rom. 8:1). If we love God and believe His Word to be true, we will be free from guilt and sin.

Don't hate yourself or your body—or your God, for that matter.

Though I had an all-consuming desire to have children, God revealed to me that it was never my "right" to bear children. He makes promises in His Word, but He never promises that we will reproduce. Instead, in the Psalms He says that He "gives the barren woman a home, making her the joyous mother of children" (113:9). He showed me that if it weren't for the pain of infertility or loss that some of us struggle through, far fewer orphans would be placed in loving homes. To date, there are estimates of over 145 million of these adoptable children in the world!

Perhaps too God, in His mercy, spares the woman who cannot bear children from a fate worse than infertility. He knows all about us. There may be reasons beyond our ability to understand that we may never experience biological motherhood. Maybe our bodies would not be able to handle the physical demands of pregnancy or childbirth. Perhaps there are potential medical conditions or illnesses carried in ours and our spouse's combined genes that would result in a child that would suffer beyond that which he or she and we could bear. What I am sure of is that I wasted far too much time and energy beating myself up and indulging in resentment of others over what I viewed as my physical and spiritual defects.

In addition to all this, it humbles me to consider the possibility that the adoption of my children has far more to do with God's plan for their lives than with my desire to have given birth to them.

I know that God wanted my children here to be raised by my husband and me for His reasons. Of that I have no doubt. We are the imperfect vehicles that He has used to place our children right where He wants them to live for reasons that only He understands. My proof is God's Word, which tells us, "And he made from one man every nation of mankind. . . having determined allotted periods and the boundaries of their dwelling place" (Acts 17:26).

Though I met with a counselor during my struggle to become a mother, I believe that I relied too heavily on family and friends for compassion and support. I shared too much with them, cried too many tears in their presence and left myself vulnerable to them as a problem to "fix."

If I had to do it all again—and, thank God, I don't—I would find a support group of other infertile couples. They are the people who understand the pain of childlessness when the hurt of it is overwhelming. Most fertility clinics provide information on these groups and on how we can get connected with them.

I am not opposed to fertility interventions, despite my experiences and my faith. But I do think that those who wish to have treatment should be educated, assertive and prayerful about any methods that they seek.

Healing Questions

1. What has been the most painful part of your infertility journey?

2. Do you harbor any unwillingness to forgive yourself, God or others for your infertility?

3. Which insights or tools from this chapter will help you to move forward with healing from the pain and grief you've experienced?

2

We Here Just Trust God for Pregnancies

Parenthood is, admittedly, highly compatible with the Christian life. Churches welcome babies with joy and gladness, parenting being a natural development of marriage.

Psalm 127:3 affirms the role of parents: "Children are a heritage from the Lord, the fruit of the womb a reward." Beyond this, countless passages detail for us how to raise children and operate within the framework of family.

My dear aunt, a great-grandmother when she died, took this perspective further. She used to say, "It's selfish not to have kids." She believed that there was no point in getting married without going forth and multiplying.

Married and wrestling with infertility when I would hear her say this, I never did debate the issue with her. Rather, obsessed with having a baby, I wanted to tell her that it can be selfish to want children more than anything else.

Not all Christians want the same things, of course. All of us probably know Christian couples who are childless by choice—and not necessarily for wrong reasons. It may be that they accept an inability to conceive and do not feel led to pursue doctors or adoption. Perhaps they are called to a demanding ministry for which they wouldn't be able to maintain the required energy and focus if they had additional family responsibilities.

Whatever their reasons, for many childless couples experiencing infertility in the context of church can be particularly painful. Babies seem to be all around those of us who attend church, a constant reminder of our seeming exclusion from God's gift and His favor.

One of every six couples experiences some form of infertility. But the human desire to raise children is so strong that Americans spend two billion dollars annually on reproductive technologies in the hopes of having babies. As an infertile woman who is also a Christian, I needed to know what God thinks about the use of fertility treatments to help women conceive.

The leadership at my church frowned on the use of them, period. But the topic of fertility intervention covers a huge amount of territory. It ranges from the use of mild hormones and removal of obstructive cysts to ovary transplants and surrogacy. I wanted to understand why my church took the stance it did without offering an explanation for its point of view. I began to suspect that because of the confusing, complicated and far-ranging implications of intervention and technology that exist, even churches that are open to some types of interventions do not have enough information to effectively counsel couples about these methods.

As I waited on the Lord to make me a mother, I often thought about Abraham and Sarah from the Bible. God had first promised them a son when Sarah was around sixty-five years old—well beyond childbearing age. But over the years Sarah grew tired of waiting for God to fulfill His promise of descendants for Abraham. In her frustration and impatience, she decided to take matters into her own hands and let her servant Hagar sleep with Abraham. She reasoned that this would once and for all provide her husband a child to carry on his name. Hagar did bear her employer's child, but after the boy's birth things didn't go quite as Sarah might have planned.

God was not pleased with Sarah's decision. He disapproved of her form of surrogacy—the process by which one woman bears a child for another . And, as we often see today, the tension between the woman who had desired the child and the one who had borne him mounted.

Hagar essentially developed an attitude toward Sarah soon after she discovered her pregnancy. Sarah in turn became a little abusive toward Hagar. Fed up, Hagar eventually left the residence.

Soon after that, though, God appeared to Hagar and made it quite clear to her that her son, born of human intervention, never had been the one planned for Abraham and Sarah—not even close. In fact, God told her, "You are pregnant. . . . You shall call his name Ishmael. . . He shall be a wild donkey of a man, his hand against everyone and everyone's hand against him, and he shall dwell over against all his kinsmen." (Gen. 16:11–12).

In Muslim teachings the Islamic prophet Muhammad, writer of the Koran, is said to be a direct descendant of Ishmael. As a Christian, I can appreciate how this surrogacy plan to produce a child went terribly wrong for all involved, and the difficulty continues today in many cases. Stories such as this may have caused the church I attended good reason to discourage people from doing that which it felt God alone should do.

Each year our minister performs a prayer service dedicated to couples trying to conceive. When one such service rolled around, my husband and I stood with six other couples, trusting God to answer our prayers. But before our pastor prayed, he gave us an update from the previous year's prayer service: All but one couple who had longed for the blessing of a baby had received. Not only this, but every couple had had a son. This was even more miraculous, the pastor told us, because boys have a greater chance of being miscarried than do girls. The one exception was a particular couple that already had a special needs child and had determined that their exclusive focus should be on him.

Our pastor's comments, however, stung me. I knew that God answered prayer. And I was truly glad for the couples who had received children following our pastor's prayer for them. Still, I wondered, how could our pastor seem so certain that his prayers would result in babies for every one of us? What about those of us who hadn't become pregnant after countless prayers for a baby and who sought medical care for help in this area?

Admittedly, at this time we were seeing a fertility specialist. We did have faith in God's ability to allow me to conceive, but I still suffered from endometriosis, since a second surgery to "clean things up" in my reproductive system had not produced the hoped-for results, and so my age combined with the damage done from the endometriosis required that I be under a doctor's care. I believed that God gives people the capability to become doctors. If I needed a wisdom tooth pulled or a pacemaker inserted, wouldn't I go to a doctor and have the procedure done to alleviate pain or prevent further physical harm?

While some churches teach that we must rely on God alone to heal us of everything, most accept medical advances to prevent, treat and cure illness and disease. Our church was of the second persuasion. So why would our leadership have a problem with God using my doctor to potentially "restore to [me] the years that the locust [had] eaten" (Joel 2:25, KJV); namely that locust called endometriosis, which had robbed me of my fertility?

The main distinction between fertility intervention and other types of medical treatment is that one assists in conceiving life while the others assist in saving or improving the quality of life.

I had to ask myself over and over again if, when it comes to conception, God disapproved of man's helping it along. Was I a bad Christian for even wondering?

This internal wrangling over what God might find acceptable or unacceptable wore me out.

Other women in my church had spoken to me about their own doctors and their use of mild forms of fertility intervention. They all had eventually become pregnant. But when it came to more aggressive and invasive procedures, which I seemed to require, no one seemed to have answers.

One morning I found out that our minister had planned a question-and-answer session with our ladies' Bible group. I thought that asking him about fertility treatments might once and for all give me some solid answers.

About fifteen minutes into the session, there was a pause. Tentatively, I raised my hand. "How might God view fertility interventions?" I asked him.

The couple of seconds that ticked by before his response seemed to me an eternity. "We here just trust God for pregnancies," he answered.

The room was graveyard silent. I felt my heart race. There had to be somebody else who wondered too. Somebody please say something, was all I could think.

I glanced around the room in a panic. I saw one mother who had taken drugs to help her ovulate. Another to get regular menstrual cycles. And across the room sat at least one who had undergone artificial insemination. Hadn't they all engaged in some form of intervention? Why were they so silent?

If I couldn't find satisfactory answers from my church, then I would find them myself with the Holy Spirit's insight. After all, God has given each of us a mind and an intellect. I thought about His invitation in Isaiah 1:18, "Come now, let us reason together."

As I began my research, right away many of the issues surrounding reproductive technologies alarmed me, especially those regarding the procedures apparently necessary for me to conceive, such as in vitro fertilization.

IVF is the process by which an egg is fertilized outside the mother's womb and the resulting embryo is implanted into her uterus. I discovered that most clinics, which are generally unregulated, usually place several embryos into a woman's uterus at once, and this can result in high-risk pregnancies of multiple babies. Nadya Suleman, the single and unemployed "Octomom" who has fourteen IVF babies at home, is a case in point.

Not only this, but excess embryos are stored away globally in cryopreservation tanks. Estimates place the number of these "frozen people" awaiting their fate at near 600,000.

I was encouraged by my doctor to use donor eggs. But psychologically and spiritually, the concept of carrying and raising an engineered child from my husband and a strange woman left me no peace.

Only after I discovered the various risks and challenges of fertility treatments did I feel a deep conviction to quit pursuing this option.

As the years passed, eventually my husband and I were led to adopt. Our church prayed for us while we were in Vietnam and China receiving our babies. When we returned home, the church members welcomed our little ones into the congregation. But one Sunday, from the very pulpit in which they had prayed for our babies, one of our pastors delivered a sermon, part of which went like this:

> The answer isn't going into poor countries and adopting a child and taking it out of his or her environment! No! We're not doing a country any justice by doing that. What we need to do is go into that country and share the gospel and show the people there how to change their lives and to transform their countries and their children!

What Hurts

I had expected that our minister's experience in leading annual prayer services for infertile couples would have provided him with compassion for how infertility feels. And I believed that my question to him merited discussion. It surprised me to have received such an abrupt answer. His reply, "We here just trust God for pregnancies," came across to me as his having drawn a line in the sand. There was "we," referring to those in the church, and then there was me, who was obviously not in line with everybody else.

I felt shame and reproach. He may as well have said, "You have no faith," because that is what I heard in my vulnerable and confused state of mind as I struggled for a godly conclusion about fertility treatments.

It would have made all the difference to me had our minister said something like, "It sounds as if you're struggling with this issue, so maybe we can talk another time," or, "I don't know, but I'd like to help you find out."

I don't expect spiritual leaders to have answers to every one of life's questions. And perhaps I was barking up the wrong tree asking this question of an elderly minister who likely saw fertility interventions as the stuff of science fiction. But I felt dismissed, and it hurt.

Many churches address issues such as substance abuse, divorce and bereavement. My church too provided ministries led by educated, compassionate leaders that were designed to help people heal from problems such as these. Why then would a minister imply that infertility demonstrates a lack of trust in God rather than considering it an important issue to discuss?

In the case of the sermon that mentioned adoptions, I understood that the message conveyed was one of drawing attention to the importance of missions work. But I wondered if elevating missions had to be done at the expense of international adoption.

Adoption may not be the ultimate transformative power in addressing the issues of poverty, hopelessness and the great need for Christ in countries across the globe. Yet it certainly does speak volumes to the child who would be dead if you hadn't showed up.

In fact, I'm almost sure our son would have died if we hadn't adopted him.

Over breakfast in the hotel the morning after we had arrived in Vietnam, the only other couple we had traveled with was told, "Your son almost died."

My husband and I were shocked by the nonchalance with which this terrible news was tossed out by our adoption facilitator. We stole nervous glances at the other couple who, for various reasons, had already endured a great deal of personal heartache up to this point.

The facilitator explained that the baby was better and that they should not worry. She told them that because he'd had parents planning to adopt him, it had been decided that he be brought to a hospital in Ho Chi Minh City for better medical care instead of being placed in a rural hospital close to the orphanage. This superior medical facility had housed four other babies from the same orphanage, all sick with a bronchial infection.

After explaining these details, our facilitator suddenly said to the couple, "Oh, sorry, not your baby." She turned to my husband and me and corrected herself. "Yours," she said.

"And four other babies in that hospital all died," she added.

It is true that missionaries do awesome work for the Lord, and they fulfill the biblical mandate to go and preach the gospel throughout the world (see Matt. 28:19). But adoption too is a fulfillment of God's Word. In James 1:27 it is said, "Religion that is pure and undefiled before God, the Father, is this: to visit orphans and widows in their affliction..." God does not specify which orphans we are to care for or say that we should exclude those outside our national borders.

There are a number of internationally adopted children who affect their native countries in positive ways. Who can say whether one or both of my children may one day reside in their birth countries and evangelize those who do not know the Lord?

And what if my children had not been in Sunday school class but sitting beside me in church the day those words were spoken? What kind of impression would they have made on my children's minds? It is wrong to discredit one biblical mandate on behalf of another.

Grace Given

Grace is necessary for those who are entrusted with teaching and preaching the Word of God. Ministers bear a heavy responsibility as they direct others in important life decisions. As they fulfill their calling, I am sure they are often keenly aware of others' disappointment in them.

I do not know to what extent most churches are equipped to counsel people on the issues of infertility and reproductive technologies. To what extent should we expect them to be? It's got to be difficult for a church to give wise, compassionate, Bible-based counsel as to how an infertile couple should join medicine with faith and prayer. After all, spiritual leaders are doctors of the soul, not the body (although God does at times override medical doctors and heal bodies through the church's prayers). Today's technologies for creating and altering life are growing at such an exponential rate, sprinting past even the courts' abilities to keep up with them. How can we expect the church to know for certain what is best for us to do?

The church is responsible for helping us apply God's Word to our lives. Since the Bible doesn't reference modern fertility treatments and interventions and points to God as the sole Creator of life, how can they not be given grace when confronted with fertility issues?

As for the sermon that in my mind cast aspersions on adoption, grace is necessary for the pastor who delivered it. As one who heads up mission trips in my church, I understand that his message was meant to encourage the congregation to see the importance and goals of missions ministry.

It is also true that a large number of countries that mission teams visit don't allow international adoptions. Even if they did, it would be virtually impossible for us to rescue from these countries every child in danger of famine and disease. As such, it is necessary for us to go to these places in order to share the gospel with their people.

I think that the main concept the minister may have been trying to communicate is a common one: "If you give a man a fish, you feed him for a day, but if you teach him to fish, you feed him for a lifetime."

Going into all the world and spreading the gospel transforms hearts and lives. Combining the Word with practical things such as providing building materials, teaching people skills and helping communities better provide for their needs fulfills biblical mandates.

Handling It

Yet we often expect much more than this from the church and its seasoned followers of Christ. If your church can't help you with some of the confusing questions you may have regarding infertility and reproductive technologies, find other sources such as support groups or books and articles. Don't be afraid to "eat the chicken and spit out the bones" when it comes to information that you come across, because you have a Bible, prayer and the Lord to guide you.

Glean what you can and then use scripture as the lens through which you understand--as well as through prayer and by seeking God's leading as He opens and closes doors for you to walk through. And He will lead. Isaiah 48:17 (NIV) says, "I am the LORD your God, who teaches you what is best for you, who directs you in the way you should go."

Don't be afraid to ask questions about your church's views on medical interventions. Find out if it has issues with any of them. After all, you're seeking clarity from the place where you expect to mature spiritually and to minister to others in order to make the best godly decisions possible.

Choose wisely the people with whom you will discuss these matters. And lower your expectations of those who put you off or give you pat answers. Sometimes what comes across as disapproval really means, "I don't understand this, so I'm not able to deal with it."

Stay strong! There are others like you out there.

Healing Questions

1. Have you ever felt conflicted by fertility treatments and your faith? Where have you turned for answers? Who or what has been most helpful to you in this area ?

2. Has anyone in ministry ever let you down when you have sought guidance from him or her? How could you respond to such a disappointment in a godly way?

3. After reading this chapter what conclusions have you reached as to how you will proceed with trying to conceive or perhaps adopting?

3

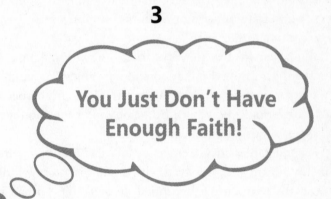

You Just Don't Have Enough Faith!

"Nope," she said as she shook her head.

"Nope, what?" I asked a trusted family friend, the shock like a punch to the gut.

"You just said, 'When I have children . . . ,' and you're not having any."

"Why would you say that?" I wanted to know.

"You're too selfish," she answered.

I suppose my crisis of faith began then, when I was a teen. Little did I know at the time that those words would haunt me for years to come.

Then as a college student, I received that diagnosis of endometriosis and had major surgery to remove half my ovaries. I began to wonder, *Is this what happens to selfish girls who aren't meant to have babies? They develop horrible diseases that spread throughout their reproductive systems and are told that their chance at conception looks bleak unless they start a family right away?*

It seemed a dark omen the third time my faith became tested on this issue, and for this occurrence I take responsibility. In my quest to better understand myself and the path my life should take, I decided in my mid-twenties to see an astrologer. Not a Christian yet, I had been fascinated with the subject of astrology and how I could apply it to my life for better self-awareness and success.

"Uh-oh," said the astrologer, an odd fellow, perhaps in his mid-forties, who began our session with the announcement that I had killed him in a former life.

"You have two areas to worry about," he informed me. "Those would be the areas of elimination and reproduction," he told me.

I felt stunned. How could he know? I had already been diagnosed with irritable bowel syndrome on top of the endometriosis. I left there with my mind in a fog.

I waited tables in Greenwich Village, New York, dreamed about my future and, involved with a late-night crowd, drank a lot. And the years ticked by until I decided that I'd had it with the alcohol and the late nights and serving cappuccinos to tourists who did not tip.

The Lord was getting a hold of me, calling me to Himself. Little by little I surrendered to Him. I packed up all my astrology and New Age books and got rid of them. I got myself a Bible. Three weeks after my thirtieth birthday, I put down the drink and never touched it again. I stopped going out at night. I took a course in crisis counseling and began to help others. But even in the midst of my new spiritual life, I was already having another crisis of faith.

For what would be a period of seven years, I had what I refer to as the baby and pregnancy dreams. Night after night I was plagued with the most horrible of nightmares. I dreamed of sick babies, dead babies at the foot of my bed, strange, bizarre, precocious babies. I also dreamed that I was pregnant a lot of the time. But just as I was about to give birth, the dream would end or I would not be able to deliver the baby. These images were so vivid and so real to me that they often woke me in the wee hours in a sweat. I can remember how I lay in my bed one night and told myself, "I will never have children." I felt this certainty to the very core of my being. Was it the devil? A lack of faith? My history? Those dreams? Was it a combination of one or more?

Then as suddenly as they had begun, the dreams stopped. It wasn't without some effort on my part, though. I made a commitment to the Lord, was baptized and spent much time in the Scriptures and in prayer for relief.

When I met and married my husband a few years later, I was eager to start a family right away. I became distraught when he told me that he wanted to wait at least a year before we tried to get pregnant. It had been more than fifteen years since my surgery, and now I was in the even less-fertile category of being over thirty-five years old. I didn't have time to waste! Plus, there they were, deeply etched in my mind, all those words—"You'll not have children," "It's selfish *not* to have children," "Have a baby *now*"—torturing me along with the dreams and the restless nights that had plagued me for years.

How do experiences such as surgery, hurtful and misinformed words spoken into one's life, ungodly ventures and nightmares about a desire of the heart affect one's faith?

The Bible tells us that "with God all things are possible" (Matt. 19:26). After I became a Christian and accepted the Lord into my life, I believed this. I saw God at work in my life, bringing about that which had seemed impossible: ending those dreams, giving me a wonderful husband and a whole host of other things. But when it came to getting pregnant, did I not have enough faith?

Apparently there were those who thought not. I have literally had friends sit on my couch with their children as they multitasked breast-feeding, wiping a nose and tying a pair of little shoes declare to me, "You just don't have enough faith in God to get pregnant!" I have sobbed on the shoulders of others during my one year, then two years of failed attempts at conception and heard, "Well, if you just had a little more faith . . ."

I've even witnessed a friend rub her swollen belly with a smile and proudly announce to me, "See, I had faith that God would give me a baby, and He has!"

What Hurts

Words spoken into our lives can hurt. The Bible says that "death and life are in the power of the tongue" (Prov. 18:21). Negative, hurtful words can do more damage than a physical injury or cause greater agony than the tremendous pain I suffered each month before my surgery in college. They can stick with us, haunt us in our darkest hours and affect our faith when we are new believers in Christ.

As a young Christian, I too wanted that great faith I saw in others. I wanted the kind that would allow me to become pregnant.

I can remember some pretty ridiculous conversations that I had with other believers in which I told them, "I know that I need more faith, but how did you do it? How did you squeeze out more faith to get what you've got?" They would usually tell me that they had believed and prayed.

"But I believe and pray!" was my answer.

"Apparently not enough," was the response.

"So how do I believe more to get more faith?" I asked.

"You just ask God to help you."

"But I do ask. I do pray."

"Well, maybe not enough."

Conversations like these would make me feel as if we were going around in circles as I chased after this elusive thing called faith that I wanted so much.

Telling people that they lack faith can feel to them as if you have just hit them over the head with a brick that has a note of condemnation tied to it. That's because Christians can so easily turn faith into *work*. But faith is not a work or an art or a skill. In fact, it doesn't even come from us. Ephesians 2:8–9 states, "For by grace you have been saved through faith. And this is not your own doing; it is the gift of God, not a result of works, so that no one may boast." Hebrews 12:2 (KJV) tells us that it is Jesus who is "the author and perfecter of our faith." He is the One who not only provides us with faith but who also perfects it as we grow in Him.

Jesus did not condemn His disciples for their lack of faith. In Matthew 17:20 we see that Jesus told them that they lacked faith when they had failed to drive a demon from a boy, and He also said to them, "I say to you, if you have faith like a grain of mustard seed, you will say to this mountain, 'Move from here to there,' and it will move."

The mustard seed at that time was the smallest particle known to man. Even tiny faith seems to be okay with the Lord. What the statement "You just don't have enough faith!" implies is that a person has no faith or that he or she must work harder to get more faith. Neither is true of the Christian.

It is all too easy for people to talk about faith when they have what they want. And it's really insensitive to lord that over someone whose desires remain unfulfilled. It isn't through human power that the right amount of faith can be summoned to make God do anything.

But there is also an element of people in the Christian community who abide by the decree that if you name it, you claim it. These are people who believe that anything they ask of the Lord will come to pass. This too is not truth. While we ought to speak positive, biblical truths into our lives and into the lives of others, God is sovereign. There are some things that no amount of claiming or faith or belief will bring to pass.

Grace Given

It has been essential for me to give grace to and forgive those who have spoken negative, ungodly words into my life about my having children. From the family friend who told me I was too selfish to have children to my dear aunt who said it is selfish not to have children to the quirky astrologer to those who have told me I lack faith to myself even, for believing in lies, grace and forgiveness have been so important. If I had not extended grace, I would be imprisoned by resentment, anger and pain. I would not have been able to maintain healthy relationships with these people or to pray for them in their struggles without having forgiven them.

I have to give grace too to those who have meant to encourage me in my faith in Christ but at the same time have been insensitive or biblically "off." We are all in different places in our walks with the Lord, and not everyone we come across has a mature faith. And while not everyone is gifted in the way he or she seeks to motivate and encourage other believers, all of us are supposed to try.

Oftentimes we encounter Christians who consider faith a work and who also overlook the need for more information about a person's heart or past before they make a pat statement about that person's necessity for greater faith. Or these believers assume that if God provided for them through their faith in Him, then there isn't any reason why He won't do the same for us.

For instance, I was once involved with a very legalistic church whose members took very seriously the notion that faith in God would heal a person of anything. One young woman suffered a great deal with anorexia. She was told not to seek help outside the church because God would heal her. After all, she was now a new creature in Christ and no longer needed to starve herself because, of course, God did not want that for her life. Yet this woman could not overcome her disease without medical intervention. Her condition got so bad that her parents came to the church and took her home for treatment. But grace is necessary even for those who are unable or unwilling to see that some of us need doctors and intervention and healing along with faith in God.

Handling It

What a person really needs sometimes is prayer, faith and some form of professional assistance. It is the same with grace and forgiveness; sometimes, even after we have forgiven someone, we need additional kinds of healing. There are moments in life when it just isn't enough for us to tell ourselves that we will let someone off the hook for their hurtful words and that we will forgive and move on. Because of my long history of not being a Christian and the things I had let into my life, and because of my propensity to obsess or to dwell on things a bit too much, after I became a Christian I needed both spiritual and emotional intervention to help me with the process of forgiveness. Sometimes we need to revisit the past, talk about things and put our hurts in proper perspective before we can move on.

In circumstances like mine, good Christian counsel can work wonders. The Lord heard my prayers for a good counselor and directed me to an excellent therapist with whom I worked for a number of years to help me heal from my ungodly past.

Another addition to grace and forgiveness that is controversial but sometimes necessary is spiritual warfare. I allowed a number of unsavory things into my life before becoming a believer in my thirties. From New Age beliefs to astrology to excessive drinking to visiting a fortune-teller to playing with a Ouija board, these things that were not of the Lord may have been a gateway for some of the oppression and skewed beliefs that developed in my mind and heart. As a Christian, simply put, I had to confess these things to God. I had to dig them up—which was painful—and ask forgiveness from the Lord for partaking in them. I then had to rebuke them and claim that they no longer had power over my life. In releasing the lies I had believed about myself, I was able to make more room in my heart for faith to take over. And what Christian doesn't want greater faith in almighty God?

One thing I do know is that a test of faith begets more faith. As I look back on some of the lowest points in my Christian life, I know that the struggles and tears that those difficulties brought produced some of my closest moments to the Lord. In my times of desperation and crisis, God has always come through. For that reason, situations that seemed hopeless to me are now sweet memories of God's hand in my life.

It's important for us to share our experiences or our testimonies with one another, because perhaps by hearing how God met us at the brink of despair, others will see how trusting in Him always results in His working all things together to the good (see Rom. 8:28).

When suffering reproach for a lack of faith, it's helpful to remind the ones reproaching us that we need only that "mustard seed of faith" to move mountains. God does not hit us over the head in our pain and despair, and His children shouldn't do it to one another either.

If we are going to confront someone about his or her faith, we should do it in love, make sure the message is specific and comes straight from the Lord to that person and perhaps give scriptural references to make things clear.

It has taken me a long time to understand how to take an insensitive remark and flip it into a positive. I can pray that God will help me to forgive another if there was any hurtful intent in his or her remark and that God will show that person how to be more sensitive to someone experiencing a pain that he or she may never know. I can ask God to increase my faith, and I can search my heart for ways in which I doubt Him and ask Him to help me trust Him. I can simply heed His words, "Be still, and know that I am God" (Ps. 46:10).

My husband and I have our family now; but were someone to tell me again that I have never borne a child because I lacked faith, even though I might still feel an initial sting from the words, I do have a ready response. I would tell that person that adoption is the vehicle by which God chose to make me a mother and that I have faith that He gave me my particular children for His reasons. I would also let them know that it took more faith than I ever thought I could have to go through our first adoption journey and to come out on the other side holding my son on US soil.

I am humbled by the realization that my past mistakes and the time it took me to heal from them have led to my having the husband and children who are now in my life. I could not imagine my life without them. What the Enemy meant for evil God has turned into good (see Gen. 50:20).

Healing Questions

1. How has your faith that you will become a parent been tested?

2. How have you handled any personal crisis of faith you have been through?

3. What painful words or experiences have stuck with you and affected your faith that God will allow you to become a parent?

4

Now You'll Get Pregnant!

According to the cheerful Emily, our adoption coordinator, my husband and I were to travel to China to adopt a baby girl in about a year. It seemed an eternity away.

That is one of the reasons I cannot forget that Saturday morning in June. Out of bed before my husband, I answered the phone as it rang. Emily's sunny voice greeted me with extra enthusiasm. Then she asked, "How would you like to go to Vietnam instead of China for a baby?"

Vietnam? I wondered, not without a little distaste. All I knew about Vietnam was the Vietnam War. Emily explained that a little boy of about four months of age was in need of a family. *A boy?* I thought, disappointed at first. *What about the baby girl I had always envisioned?*

But what caught my attention was the timing: if John and I were to accept the referral for this baby boy, our trip to Vietnam was scheduled to take place in six weeks. The idea of me becoming a mother in just a month and a half seemed so tantalizing, so incredible; I began to imagine myself with a son instead of a daughter. I yelled for John to wake up.

John walked down the stairs in his bathrobe and looked alarmed. As I explained the conversation to him, Emily waiting on the phone, he seemed downright shocked. As he struggled to absorb it all, Emily told me, "I'll send you the baby's photo."

Mad with excitement and curiosity, I ran to the computer while John took the phone to talk with Emily.

At the time, we had a PC in an upstairs office. I downloaded the image Emily had sent us and printed it out to show John.

The printer chugged and chugged until an entire page filled itself with the image of an infant's face. My infant's face—because I knew in a matter of an instant that this little boy was meant to be mine.

And so it was that we accepted the referral, and our adoption plans began in earnest. However, since we had expected that it would be another year before we traveled to adopt in China, we were still attempting fertility intervention to conceive a child and were about to undergo our second round of artificial insemination (AI).

Most of our family and friends were unaware of this new attempt at AI. I had learned by now not to leave myself vulnerable to a lot of questions and to have to share the devastating news if our efforts were unsuccessful. Yes, I focused on the upcoming adoption with excitement, but I had already taken all the drugs and hormones to complete this round of AI. Besides, I wanted to keep all my options open and let God lead. Perhaps I would adopt a baby boy in Vietnam and become pregnant, maybe with a girl. I just didn't know—until that second round of AI.

Apart from the abrupt and almost disdainful stand-in who performed the procedure for me that day in place of our regular warm and wonderful specialist, something in my heart told me that this attempt too would be unsuccessful. I felt the sting of failure and emptiness before the insemination even began. Was it a nudge from God to say that we were meant to parent this baby boy in Vietnam and not one from my own body, or was it the Enemy whispering to me that I did not deserve a biological child?

Either way, after this I tried hard to lay to rest my dream to birth a child. I never anticipated, however, that speaking to others about our plans to adopt would resurrect my desire to conceive time and again.

It is interesting how often a woman who begins pursuing adoption is told, "Now you'll get pregnant!" In other words, "Now that you've stopped trying, your desires will be fulfilled." Many women in the adoption process feel a strange mixture of emotions wash over them when they hear those words. I know I did: hope, despair, anger and confusion.

The hope I felt stemmed from the possibility that God was speaking through those who so confidently made this statement— that they discerned a reality I did not see. The confused part of me felt that perhaps adoption was not the path we should take; maybe we were calling it quits on a successful pregnancy too soon.

At the same time I despaired and felt anger over the fact that what people imparted to me happened to be a false sense of hope. After all, no one knew my body the way I did or had experienced my journey through infertility and reproductive medicines. It further upset me to think that all this banter about me becoming pregnant might be intended to negate adoption as the vehicle by which I was meant to become a mom. Did they mean to imply that somehow adopting a child wasn't as good a thing as bearing a biological child? And oh, did I ever love that baby boy whom I had never met! At this point I had a stronger sense of God leading me to become this child's mother than I did that I would conceive.

The only thing I knew for sure was that the excitement with which people seemed to anticipate my "inevitable" pregnancy was a bit disarming for me.

I remember a conversation I had at this time with a close friend. I told her of our referral for our baby boy in Vietnam as well as our second attempt at conception through artificial insemination. As we chatted, she stopped the conversation. "Wait a minute," she said. We both paused for a brief moment.

"Does this adoption referral mean that you are praying that the artificial insemination won't work?" she asked.

"Of course not," I replied, a bit taken aback by her question.

"So are you praying that the adoption won't go through and that the AI will work?" she continued.

"No," I told her, with an ache in my heart at the thought that the referral might not go through. "I just want God to choose one or both or neither for me, based on His will for my life."

While my friend still seemed confused, I had just experienced a moment of epiphany. With the picture of our intended son in front of me and that instant, inexplicable love for him that had grabbed hold of me the moment I received that photo, I knew that I could not bear the thought that I might lose him. I realized now that I did not care if the AI worked or not—not really. I cared about the son I already had. So all those times that I had been told I would get pregnant after I received the referral for my son had been like a woman already with child hearing how exciting it will be when she does conceive.

What Hurts

An adoption process is like a pregnancy. Adoptive parents are in a state of anticipation and preparation. They make plans for how they will receive and parent their new family, imagine their future, try out baby names, take care of their health and count down the weeks until the baby or child comes. When people tell them that now they'll be expecting when they already are, it feels to them as if it's a slight to the precious life that already exists, to the child they are waiting to bring home.

Since the statement "Now you'll get pregnant!" does give false hope to a woman who is desperate to have a baby, unless a person has been in direct and definitive contact with the Lord that the adoptive woman will conceive, people must not toy with a woman that way. She is too vulnerable. Sometimes her thoughts and judgment are clouded, and such a statement makes her think that maybe, just maybe, she too will find favor with God and conceive and bear one of those miracle babies. After all, she is told that it happened to a friend's cousin's sister-in-law, and an ex-coworker's brother's wife and a woman whom a friend went to church with three moves ago . . .

It is such a tired cliché, a favorite folktale, to say that adoption is somehow a cure for infertility. RESOLVE, the US-based National Infertility Association, states, "First, it suggests that adoption is only a means to an end, not a happy and successful end in itself. Second, it is simply not true."[1] Some experts say that 3 to 10 percent of couples will become pregnant after adopting, which is the same number as couples who will conceive after discontinuing fertility treatments and not pursuing adoption. Additionally, the idea that a couple will become pregnant once the pressure is off to conceive and they begin to pursue adoption is also largely erroneous. Fertility specialists place the number of couples experiencing infertility due to stress at as little as 5 percent.

Says Danielle Pennel in her blog, *My Paperwork Pregnancies*, "I know of a handful of couples who have gotten pregnant without infertility treatments once they chose adoption. They were extremely surprised and happy," she shares. But, she adds, "some of these couples were even a bit mad that they got pregnant because they didn't want to become the 'cliché' which had annoyed them so much before."[2]

And another thing—this perspective devalues the soon-to-be adopted child. The statement implies, "You'll get what you really valued and wanted all along now that you've gone after this other thing, this adoption thing."

Grace Given

In my own experience, I have learned that there are many women who actually do conceive right before, during or after an adoption. Only God knows just why, and perhaps there is a speck of truth to the adage, "Once you stop trying to get the thing you want, you will receive it." I think the comment comes from people who know someone in their lives for whom a miraculous pregnancy became a reality. It may also stem from the knowledge that a woman who says this knows what it is like to make unsuccessful attempts to become a mother or have watched a friend go through such grief and heartache and wants to encourage her and offer hope. But even with some of these "miracle" pregnancies, everything does not always turn out to be rosy, and grace and forgiveness are more important than ever.

Take, for instance, friends of my husband and mine, Cathy and Jarrod. After years of unsuccessful fertility treatments, they decided to pursue a China adoption. With the process well underway, having completed the reams of paperwork required, been fingerprinted, undergone background checks and a home study, Cathy discovered that she was pregnant. Unlike many couples who are happy to forgo the time and expense associated with international adoption when they learn they are pregnant, such was not the case with Cathy and Jarrod. Though they were thrilled with a completely unexpected pregnancy, they felt a great sense of responsibility for and connection to the child they had been imagining for months, the one they had already named, loved, prayed about and in many ways prepared for. In their minds, to halt the adoption proceedings would be to let their adopted daughter down as well as to miss out on a blessing in their lives. So they decided to allow God to doubly bless them.

When it came time for the couple to travel to China to pick up their new daughter, Cathy was told by her doctor that she would be unable to fly the nearly thirteen hours for the trip because she was too close to her due date. Just in the nick of time, as Jarrod returned home with sixteen-month-old Megan, Cathy went into labor with their son, Chase. Throughout her pregnancy Cathy and Jarrod decided not to be informed about the sex of their child. They wanted to be surprised when he or she arrived into the world. They just didn't anticipate being surprised over and again by Chase's presence in their lives.

Not only was Chase bestowed with the title "Miracle Baby" or "Miracle Boy" by immediate and extended family members and friends, he had the distinction of being the first son to be born into this family after a generation. The great fanfare surrounding his arrival and the attention lavished on him were wonderful responses in celebration of his new life, yet what Megan seemed to receive upon her arrival into the clan paled in comparison. A fussy baby with difficulty transitioning to her new surroundings and connecting with hoards of family descending upon the household to see Chase, Cathy says Megan was often "overlooked or ignored." She admits she also wrestled with guilt over trying to divide her time between a newborn and a new internationally adopted toddler. Recovering from a C-section from Chase's birth didn't help matters much either. "I couldn't lift Megan for a long while," she says, "and neither of my babies slept through the night, each one waking at different times. I was just so exhausted that there wasn't much in me to give her at first."

With Chase being given special treatment over Megan and the constant referral of him as a miracle in front of them, Cathy and Jarrod got mad. They told me that they really did feel hurt that their loved ones and friends seemed to consider Chase as the "prize" and Megan as some sort of "charity case." One of her family members even asked Cathy why they had even bothered with the adoption when they got what they had wanted all along.

"We decided it all had to stop," says Cathy. "We insisted that everybody stop calling Chase a miracle in front of Megan when after all, she was a miracle in her own right." They also informed others that making such a fuss over Chase being a boy was no different than what a lot of cultures and countries do when they oppress or disregard daughters. They also began, as Cathy healed and got stronger—and the kids slept through the nights—to celebrate Megan, introducing her culture into theirs and building pride in their daughter for her Chinese heritage.

"I have to admit though," shares Cathy, "that it all took a lot of patience, correcting people, setting boundaries and prayer to get through it." She adds, "It wasn't easy to forgive people for thinking of Megan as almost irrelevant, but my faith dictated that I did."

By extending grace and forgiveness to loved ones and friends, Cathy and Jarrod have preserved important relationships with people who now love both of their children. "Actually, God gave me a bird's eye view of what it's like to be female in some pretty dark places," Cathy told me. She now has a passion for women's rights and works with charities that create opportunities for girls and women worldwide. "And you know what?" she adds. "In those early days when I was kind of out of commission for a while, Megan and Jarrod built a really tight connection that they share now, years later."

Handling It

All too often adoption is looked at as a compromise or a consolation prize—even by adoptive parents who try to work through their own infertility or miscarriage issues! The reality is that not every loving, married couple is meant to conceive and raise biological offspring. Think of the thousands upon thousands of children who are already born or yet to be born who, without the blessing of adoption, would be without families, homes, nutritious food, medicine and education.

As John and I pursued the adoption of our first child, I listened but did not usually respond to people who meant well and told me that now I would become pregnant. But I felt the glow on my face and the hope in the pit of my stomach that somehow I just might experience the miracle of pregnancy, despite my endometriosis-ravaged reproductive past and "bum" eggs. But no sooner would the hope spark than both guilt and anger would wash over me. Guilt because I felt that my acceptance of what I was being told betrayed the infant son whom I knew in my heart God meant for us to receive and raise. And then anger at the person who with nonchalance had tossed out the words "Now you'll get pregnant!" for triggering hope for something other than our soon-to-be-adopted child.

John and I were clearly observing the hand of God in the orchestration of our adoption process, down to the very minute details. I knew in my heart that this journey to Vietnam would be the birth process by which I was meant to become a mother. Sure, God could have seen fit to bless me with a pregnancy on top of that. But deep down, knowing my limitations, such a gift likely would have tested me beyond what I could bear. I understand that God will never do that to one of His children.

By the time John and I embarked on our second adoption journey to get Olivia from China, I handled the "Now you'll get pregnant!" statement, which was said far less often, with a simple "It's in God's hands."

Healing Questions

1. Has anyone ever made the comment "Now you'll get pregnant!" to you after he or she found out about your adoption plans?

2. If so, how did that make you feel?

3. How could you respond to such a statement while undergoing an adoption process?

5

You Adopted, So You Can't Have Kids, Right?

Assumptions about adoption aren't just made by "outsiders" who have erroneous facts or who are ignorant about it. As adoptive couples go through the process to bring home and settle their children, we discover that we too can have our own judgments about it.

For instance, even after my husband and I returned home from Vietnam with our son Lucas, I held onto the misconception that those who adopt aren't able to bear biological children. Except for the case of older couples who want more children and shouldn't or couldn't risk another pregnancy or for those rare "miracle" babies that happened for some during or after the adoption process, I thought infertility had to be pretty much every adoptive parent's story.

Home with my son for about six months, I decided to host a get-together for some mothers I had met and their newly adopted babies. One woman I knew brought along a friend named Lori who had an adorable daughter she had adopted from China.

Happy to have opened my home to this group and to make a new friend with whom I expected I had a lot in common, I began to chat away with Lori. Then, without reservation, I asked her about her infertility story.

"I have no idea if I'm infertile or not," she responded as my face grew hot from surprise and embarrassment. "I just always knew I wanted to adopt."

In haste I apologized to her for my presumptuous and intrusive inquiry, but she brushed it off.

"That's okay," she said, shrugging her shoulders. "People ask that all the time."

So I wasn't the only one who had taken the liberty of asking about Lori's reproductive system—which I now shudder to think that I brought up with the woman five minutes after meeting her.

After this encounter I began to wonder, *If she gets questioned about infertility all the time, what must it be like for her?* I wondered if people came right out and said to her, "So what about you? Do you have blocked fallopian tubes?" or, "Does your husband have a low sperm count?" or, "Which fertility specialist have you seen?"

I felt compassion for Lori because she often faced assumptions from others about her body simply because she had chosen to adopt instead of pursuing having biological children. I realized that though she had been the recipient of my awkward blunder that day, in the end she gave me a gift. She helped me to see that not everybody who wants to be a mother is as preoccupied with her reproductive system as I had been. For Lori adoption had been a wonderful choice that she had always wanted to make.

What Hurts

God showed me through this one short encounter with Lori that what I understood about adoption was filtered through a rather self-absorbed frame of reference. Even after Lucas came home, I still found myself consumed by my infertility and by what I had missed out on in pregnancy. My question to Lori had been narrow-minded and based upon a presumption that we adoptive parents walk about carrying the same "curse."

Instead of attempting to bond with her through our shared adoption and parenting experiences, I tried to connect with her over the grief and resentment I assumed she had experienced, like me, over having a broken body.

I felt humbled, because in a moment I realized that all those things that were of crucial importance to me—the ability for my husband to carry on his name through a biological son, the longing to see a mini-me smile up at me, the ability to give birth as did millions upon millions of other women—didn't matter to Lori. She just wanted to be a mother through adoption, and she was happy.

But I had joy! I now was mother to a beautiful son for whom I had fought and whom I loved with what I thought was all my heart. Yet to my horror, there I stood with enough room in that heart and in my head for some baggage. Part of me still believed the lie that adoption was second best or a "backup plan" for what I still expected from God for my life. I had not yet completely surrendered to the Lord my desire for a pregnancy. Nor had I reached a place of total contentment with adoption as my only means of achieving motherhood. This insight caused me much pain.

My conversation with Lori ended pretty much after I questioned her infertility. In my moment of both revelation and embarrassment, I found myself too overwhelmed to continue to speak with her.

Despite her gracious response, I have to wonder if there isn't a small part of her that is annoyed by the repetitive questions asked by others about what they believe is her inability to conceive and bear children. I have to imagine that the presumption must get tiresome for her. She should not have to defend the beautiful first choice she made to become a mother through adoption. Maybe, just maybe, the frequency of inquiries she receives puts a thought or two into her head that she is somehow different or odd for the choice she has made. I hope not. I hate to think that I may have been one of those people who might have planted that seed!

Due to my ignorance, I spoke inappropriately, but God in His mercy chose to show me the error of my ways and of my heart.

Grace Given

As I said, that day at my house God gave me a gift that I believe was the product of His grace. He showed me not only that adoption is a first choice for some but also how much further I needed to go to relinquish the idea of a biological child and to fully embrace my son. For many women the pain of infertility does not just evaporate once an adoption takes place. Healing and surrender can be a slow process.

Lori offered me grace too through her gracious choice not to take issue with my questions about her fertility.

I have to give grace to myself and to anyone who mistakenly believes that if a couple wants to have children and is able to procreate, they will.

I am sure there are many out there who view adoption as I have—as a way to enlarge a family after having had biological children or as an alternative for couples who are unable to have them. It may not make sense to some that anyone would choose not to produce genetic offspring. What couple, they think, would not want to see themselves reflected in the smiles of a chubby toddler who has Daddy's curly hair or Mommy's big brown eyes? What about God's instruction in the Bible to go forth and multiply (see Gen. 9:7)? Isn't this the most natural thing in the world?

There are people I know who say that they could never love a child who did not share their genetic makeup. For these too I give grace. They have never given themselves the opportunity to see how easy and natural it is to love any child.

Handling It

Although I am glad that God exposed my bad heart attitudes of self-absorption, lack of gratitude and even of self-pity, surrender to and contentment in all things has been a process for me. It's important to remember that for those of us who profess faith in Christ, we are works in progress (see Phil. 1:6).

Have you ever played a game with your children in which you ask them what kind of animal they would like to be? The child then tells you his or her animal of choice and acts out its characteristics. It's a fun pastime with small kids, and my children have oftentimes picked out fierce, powerful animals like lions or cute and cuddly ones like kittens and puppies.

It seems to me that God sometimes plays a game like this with us, His children, only He asks us to be a vegetable—and always an onion.

Just as an onion can be peeled away layer by layer, we too must allow God to strip away our outer layers of sin, immaturity and bad heart attitudes on a continual basis. We know that God wants to get to the very core of our beings in order to heal us and transform us from the inside out. That's because so many of our outer layers block us from God's primary purpose in our lives: to conform us to the image of His Son, Jesus Christ (see Rom. 8:29). God wants to peel away every one of these layers.

I love my children, and I would die for them. They have been all that I have hoped for and more. I embrace them and know that God has orchestrated their journeys into my arms and my heart. And I have great admiration for those who, like Lori, make adoption their first choice to bring children into their lives.

But I do admit that my desires for pregnancy, giving birth, having a newborn and delighting in a child from the union of my husband and me are all things that I have had to surrender, layer by layer.

I am so grateful that I married the man God chose for me. Unlike men I dated in the past with whom I shared my infertility issues, John has never had an issue with my inability to conceive. And he has always been there to comfort me and to dry my tears through all the disappointment and heartache after our failed attempts at conception. In truth, I placed a burden on myself to bear for him a son, whereas it was never that important to him. Holding tight to John has helped me a lot.

If I think back on it, I know that in reality I did have a choice to bear a child. When my fertility specialist refused to perform in vitro fertilization on me with less than three or four of my eggs, which my ovaries would not produce, he suggested that I use donor eggs. I could have pursued this course to fulfill my desire to have a child, and I know that my husband would have supported it. The child would have been genetically his, and I could have picked a female donor as close in looks to myself as possible. The truth is, I did not want to. I believed, and still believe, that such a path was not the one God had in mind for us.

Sometimes we must remember that risky, herculean efforts to produce children may not be God's choice for our lives. Perhaps the money we would have spent on three rounds of IVF could be used to save three orphans.

I thought that once we adopted and our family was "complete," I would no longer think about what might have been. But I still did and sometimes do. I also imagined that after my experience with an early menopause, I would *finally* stop seeing, in my mind's eye, a picture of me with a protruding stomach. Well, the stomach has become a reality, but for all the wrong reasons! I thought that I would no longer wonder about how it feels to have another person grow inside of me or about that moment of delivering a new life into the world. But I did not. And for me this has been my ongoing personal struggle. Though the images have faded over the years and the desire to bear a child has dwindled through the course of time, I may always wonder. And that's OK. No matter what I feel, I know that God has His reasons for allowing it and that He will continue to strip away my layers.

But I can say that I no longer look at adoptive parents the same way and assume that their story is mine or that their choice to bring children into their lives through adoption was ever a second choice.

Healing Questions

1. What motivates you or has motivated you to want to adopt?

2. How can seeing yourself as an "onion" that is being stripped of negativity and ungodliness help you with any residual feelings that you may have regarding infertility or loss in your life?

3. How are you a work in progress right now with respect to either wanting children or having adopted them?

6

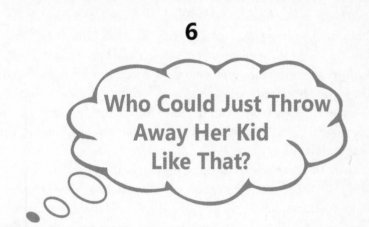

Who Could Just Throw Away Her Kid Like That?

The stereotypical birth mother who has given up her child for adoption has several different faces. But do we ever see who she really is?

In the United States she often wears too much makeup over a sullen expression. She is the young, promiscuous teen with a spotty school record and behavioral problems. She may not know who fathered her baby and may have ignored her pregnancy for a long while. She either couldn't afford an abortion or, in denial about her condition, waited too long to get one.

On the other hand, sometimes this young woman's procrastination to deal with the life inside her is intentional. Though she is terrified of her parents' reaction to her pregnancy, she holds a romantic view of what motherhood will be like. She imagines that she will receive from her baby the unconditional love that she craves. If she knows the baby's father, she hopes that he will step up to the plate and help her parent. Sadly, too often her baby's absent father and her own overburdened parents force her to give up her child. These circumstances, along with the discovery that babies don't just love but need all the time, leave her with empty arms.

We turn away from the drug-addicted young woman who hadn't even realized she was pregnant and has abandoned her baby. That's because her health and body don't receive too much of her attention. She is too focused on her next fix. In her drug-consumed hazes, she forgets any suspicions that she could be pregnant. So she goes into an early labor and delivers a premature, drug-addicted baby. It costs hundreds of thousands of dollars to nurse it to health. This child is taken away from her. She feels badly, but rather than work to get her baby back, she returns to the powerful lure of the streets and of drugs.

Pitiful and unkempt is the haggard face of the "mother by trade." She is the real-life version of the nursery-rhyme character who has all those children living in a shoe. This mother lives in government housing and collects a welfare check each month that grows proportionately with the size of her brood. None of the children's several fathers helps to support her. She and her children subsist on taxpayers' money until one more mouth to feed strains this mother beyond her physical and financial limitations, and she gives a child up. This woman either doesn't use birth control or is too fertile for contraception to work.

One of the most disturbing of our stereotypes is the one featured on the evening news. She is the fresh-faced, pretty, popular teen who gives birth in a bathroom at the school prom. After her secret delivery of a baby that nobody knew about, she leaves the newborn on the cold, dirty tile floor, adjusts her strapless gown and heads back to the party for another dance.

We ignore the lonely young woman who knows that her new boyfriend will leave her if he has to come back to the apartment and listen to a newborn wail and have it demand all her time. She loves her child, but she loves being loved more, and she chooses her boyfriend over her baby. She shoves its tiny frame into a cardboard box and leaves it in the vestibule of a building a block from her home.

Another of our stereotypes is seventeen but looks as if she is in her twenties. That's because she had to grow up fast. At first she embraced the role of mother at the tender age of fourteen. But after the second and then the third baby came, she got tired of living as an adult when she was still a teen. She decides one day to leave her kids at a bus stop.

All these scenarios have at times been, and will continue to be, reality. They stir within the hearts of the general population, in particular with those of us who struggle to have children, a righteous anger. The scales of justice are lopsided when innocent life is tossed in with a destructive mix of drugs, poverty, immaturity, endangerment and suffering.

Our anger is stirred up too over people who abandon babies in nations other than ours. Some believe that countries should provide better resources to their people. If education, birth control and access to abortion were more prevalent, they reason, fewer innocent children would be abandoned and left to die. They also surmise that in nations in which values are inconsistent with our Western thinking, baby abandonment results from placing a low value on human life, period.

Many give the Chinese harsh reviews for their abandonment of thousands of baby girls each year. Both before and after we adopted Olivia from a busy, industrial Chinese province, our friends and relatives offered us their unsolicited opinions as to why China behaves as it does. People told us, "Yeah, they get rid of babies there," or, "They don't want girls in China, so they dump 'em."

Though I couldn't bring myself to accept these brazen, negative assertions, to be sure, I was curious. It appeared that the Chinese place a lesser value on the life of a female than that of a male.

What Hurts

To expect the worst from groups or from certain types of people without having all the facts—that hurts. But eradicating stereotyping and judgment of others is difficult when the bad that we anticipate in people sometimes exists.

When we are correct in our determination of where an abandoned, neglected or harmed baby came from, it validates our already tainted thinking. And the resulting confidence in our judgment causes us to reason that we should never expect any different from certain types or groups of people.

But our expectations often sour into self-righteousness. We imagine that we and those with whom we associate function on a higher moral ground than do others in society. This serves to empty us of compassion and understanding for the promiscuous, addicted, selfish or irresponsible among us. As if we have no sin ourselves! We point a finger of blame and disgust at others, whom we shun. At the same time we do nothing to help change people and situations.

Grace Given

There are drug-addicted women for whom custody of their babies is revoked so that their infants can be protected. There are large families of children living under one roof whose birth parents are overwhelmed and overtaxed. There are countries—and this is true also of subcultures here in the United States—in which a son is preferable to that of a daughter.

No society or class of people is without its share of children born out of wedlock, teen sex, poverty and addiction.

When these conditions affect our most innocent—helpless, vulnerable infants and children—most of us become angry and emotional. If we did not, our indignation and our desire to protect these children would not motivate us to help change things. Yet all too often we feel frustrated by our limited time and means to address these kinds of social issues, so we hold onto our anger and sadness in the form of prejudice, stereotypes and hurtful words.

But we do deserve a measure of grace at times for our feelings and attitudes, because some of the acts committed against infants and children are heinous and unthinkable—and because one baby who suffers is one too many.

For a society that is fed by a daily diet of injustices and that holds onto negative attitudes, grace is necessary. We hear about these injustices instantaneously in our information age in which the messes humans make of their lives are hurtled at us one after the other. With every bit of new technology and every scientific advance, there are countless among us who connive ways to profit from and to abuse hurting people. An onslaught of the senseless, brutal things that people do to one another demands that we make some sense of life as we know it.

Our human desire to see order brought into situations of chaos can cause us to spout blanket statements into the air. Somebody has to be held accountable for the wrongs happening around us, so we make people pay with our broad generalizations, half-truths and negative language.

Though it isn't unusual for couples in their forties and even fifties to parent young children today, it is a fact that fertility diminishes with age. While many agree that teens and unmarried young women can find ways to avoid becoming pregnant, these women can't help it that they are fertile. The most fertile in our society are the youngest and oftentimes most immature—sometimes too inexperienced in life to give babies proper care and parenting. We have to give them grace too, for they live in a culture that promotes the idolatry of youth, sexual fulfillment, self-gratification and pleasure to the very ones most likely to bring new life into the world.

When my husband and I first pursued adoption, it was of the domestic kind. We found out about quite a few young women in our area who were not happy about their pregnancies. We thought that there existed the possibility of adopting one of their infants. As we began conversations with the relatives of these young women, we were stunned by what many of these girls were telling their families. The painful reality was that as these women considered their options, adoption for their babies was the least favorable outcome they saw.

When we asked why, the explanation given was that the expectant girl or woman had communicated, "I'd rather abort my baby than give it to a stranger." To me that sounded like the irrational reasoning of an obsessed lover: "If I can't have you, nobody can." It smacked of selfishness. But young people can be selfish.

The good news is that in almost every case of an unplanned pregnancy that we knew about, the biological mother made the decision to keep her child. But a huge dose of grace must be given to the young woman who makes the unselfish choice to carry a baby to term and then give it up for the good of the child.

Every time a birth mother gives up her baby, hers is a child that is not aborted. But, sad to say, there are clinics in some areas of this country that will perform an abortion on a woman during her third trimester. I know this to be true because a high school friend of mine had one such abortion. She was eight months pregnant, and that abortion, which was actually a birth, changed her forever.

God's Word says, "Greater love hath no man than this, that a man lay down his life for his friends" (John 15:13, KJV). The very nature of pregnancy and childbirth is to lay down one's life. It is a sacrifice in which anything can happen to the mother or the child.

Handling It

Besides focusing on those cases in which parents abandon, harm and kill their children, the media has played somewhat of a positive role in dispelling some of the stereotypes of birth parents who relinquish babies. There have been a few television programs on adoption that have enabled viewers to gain insight into such people. MTV's *Sixteen and Pregnant* and WE tv's *The Locator* paint intimate and accurate portraits of what young parents who give up their children for adoption are like and why they make the choice they do. Shows such as these are helpful in allaying some of our society's stereotypes of young birth parents who relinquish infants.

Thanks to open adoptions, which allow for contact between a birth parent and his or her biological child, more young women choose to give birth to their babies and place them in loving homes.

Rather than continue to wonder about the preference for boys over girls in China and make presumptions about the Chinese, I decided to do some research.

When adopting overseas, it is helpful to gain knowledge about the facts surrounding the abandonment of babies. Learning what motivates the Chinese to give up a disproportionate number of their daughters has been insightful for me and has given me compassion for those who make this choice.

According to author Matt Rosenberg in a 2012 About.com article, China instituted a one-child policy over thirty years ago. Chinese leader Deng Xiaoping established the policy in 1979 in order to limit Communist China population growth. It has largely been restricted to ethnic Han Chinese who live in urban areas. However, there are other parts of China where the one-child policy has been enforced as well.[1] So many of the people I have spoken with are unaware of this policy.

The Chinese who comply with the government policy are given special recognition and perks. Those who don't can face serious consequences. Among these are stiff fines, often too steep for the average Chinese family to pay. There are also pressures to abort a pregnancy and even forced sterilization as a result of a second pregnancy.

Coupled with this policy is the fact that the Chinese government does not dole out Social Security or other benefits to its elderly. For centuries children have been their parents' providers and caretakers when they age. It is the male child who is expected to take on this responsibility. The female child in China, once married, is not expected to care for elderly parents but helps in the care of her husband's family. A son is significant to the Chinese in terms of their own welfare when they are no longer able to work and provide an income for themselves.

One evening before John and I left for China, I found myself glued to a documentary about the enforcement of the one-child policy in China. The show filmed "medical teams" that went out in search of women who were pregnant with a second child.

I watched the team confront a woman who lived on a farm with one child and was in her eighth month of pregnancy with a second. At first they tried to persuade the woman to abort her baby. When that didn't work, they set about holding her down on a table, and they performed a forced abortion.

I don't think I will ever forget the image of this woman, helpless to prevent the death of her baby. Her cries of pain and heartbreak are forever etched in my mind.

How she was tracked down in a remote location so close to her due date remains a mystery to me. However, it is thought that there are those who will turn in a woman who is pregnant with a second child. These informants are said to be compensated for their information.

This woman's is not a unique story. Forced abortions have been performed on women in their ninth month of pregnancy. At times a woman will deliver her child, and the infant will be put to death upon its birth.

While a second child may still be illegal in some parts of China, the irony is that so too is abandonment of a child. In a country in which ultrasounds are not the routine for pregnant women, there is no way for a mother to know the sex of her child until she delivers it. Should it be a girl, there can be enormous pressure on her by her husband and family to abandon it. Thus she must take an enormous risk in placing the child in a location where it will be safe until found. Our daughter Olivia was brought to the entrance of the orphanage, where she resided for the first thirteen months of her life.

Things are changing a little in China, and this ban on second children is being lifted in some places. But the truth remains that the Chinese love their children, and many wish they could have more. I have great compassion now for Chinese birth mothers.

When I think about my children's birth parents, in particular their birth mothers, I know that they have experienced pain that I cannot ever imagine. I often wonder what they might think about the children they gave up. I'm sure they remember their birthdays. Maybe they imagine what they look like and what life is like for them now.

They carried my children for nine months, delivered them into the world and then had to say goodbye. That is a sorrow I cannot comprehend. It is so important to remember that a birth mother is not a mere statistic with a face that we may not want to see. Rather, she is a reason for a blessing in our lives. Had either abortion or infanticide been used by either of my children's mothers to eliminate them, there would be no Lucas or Olivia. Had they even used birth control, these two unique and special human beings would not exist. To me and to all whose lives they have touched and enriched, that is unimaginable.

Healing Questions

1. Have you ever held stereotypical views about birth mothers who give up their children? Which of the stereotypes listed in this chapter have you most entertained?

2. Will you or do you now think of your child's birth parents? How do you feel when you think of them?

3. What have you or will you tell your child about his or her birth parents?

PART 2

Not in Front of the Kids!

7

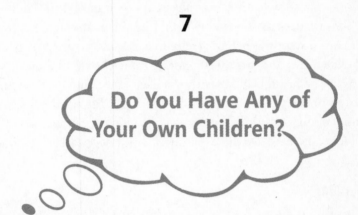

Do You Have Any of Your Own Children?

I was at a birthday party for a longtime friend, and I was getting reacquainted with some former coworkers I hadn't seen in years. We all sat on my friend's terrace, where we enjoyed a view of the Manhattan skyline.

"Do you have kids?" Jim, a former artist turned successful musician, asked.

"Sure," I said. "Would you like to see their pictures?" I felt myself beam with pride as I passed around my wallet, which contained two recent school photos of Lucas and Olivia.

"Cute," Jim said. "But do you have any of your own kids?"

"They are my own kids," I replied with a smile, while inside I felt myself seethe with anger and hurt.

Jim glanced at my husband, who sat beside me and had taken my hand in a gesture that I understood was meant both to comfort and calm me. Jim's look at John seemed to be to ensure that he hadn't overlooked any Asian traits in my husband. No one said anything until my dear sweet friend Coco, the birthday girl, gave me a sympathetic glance and said, "Of course they're her kids." Then she broke the tension. She hopped up out of her chair and asked, "Who needs another drink?"

There has got to be a better way to differentiate between biological and adopted children than by the use of this widespread phrase—that is, when it is even necessary to make a distinction.

The cavalier use of one's own children versus adopted children sets many an adoptive parent's teeth on edge—and it make us grind them when the comparison is made in front of our children.

We've all heard people say things like, "They couldn't have any children of their own, so they adopted," or, "My husband and I thought about adopting, but then we had kids of our own."

How do we receive these comments? Is it necessary to respond to them?

What Hurts

Because this book addresses adoption, the distinction between those who are adopted and those who are not is necessary and warrants clarity. Therefore, the terms "biological," "genetic," "genetically related" and "birth" are used throughout the book to describe children and parents who share DNA.

You won't find common phrases such as "one's own children" or "natural children." The latter seems to imply that there could be such a thing as "unnatural children."

There is nothing "unnatural" about children not birthed from a mother's own body or about the process of adoption to create a family. Adopted children cry real tears, eat real food, reach real developmental milestones, carry on their parents' surnames, fill in their family trees and receive family inheritances.

My children are mine, just as is any child being raised by a loving, responsible adult or adults. But we should be aware that our children are not ours for eternity. The Bible says that there will be no marriages in heaven (see Matt. 22:30), so our defined connections of "my" children and "my" spouse are but temporary and earthly, not eternal.

Referring to children as a person's own not only insults the parent and the child but neglects to give authority and recognition to the God who has orchestrated an adoption and thus formed a family.

A stranger who asks, "Do you have any of your own kids?" within earshot of your children crosses a boundary. He or she presumes that your children did not come from your body, and this person inflicts an injury on your children, who may hear that they are some kind of substitute children. And nobody has the right to know if you have other children at soccer practice or at home studying algebra, or whether you gave birth to them.

To voice this curiosity demonstrates a false sense of entitlement to information that is not anyone's business. It is insensitive and inappropriate, perhaps borne out of ignorance, to think nothing of overstepping these boundaries to violate someone's privacy. What if the roles were reversed? What if I, as an adoptive parent, walked up to a family of two parents and three children who looked similar to each other while they picnicked in a park and asked, "Do you have any children that aren't your own?" I might end up covered in their potato salad.

But adoptive parents probably would not ask such a thing, because we understand the inappropriateness of that kind of question. We know that it's hurtful and potentially harmful. Adoptive parents fear how such encounters affect our kids because we have as much of a maternal or paternal instinct to protect them as does any mother or father. It frightens and angers us when we are broadsided by the injustice of an assault on our children's identities. We belong to them, and they to us. We don't want our kids to feel anything less than a sense of security as the "real" children of "real" parents. We want the rest of society—in all the places we go and in all the things we do—to view them the same way.

Instead of saying that a couple couldn't have kids of their own, so they adopted, it might be better to leave out the three words "of their own." That's because those three little words can strike a chord within the adoptive parent, who may always remember the pain of infertility. No adoptive parent wants to be reminded of how they suffered and felt inadequate over such a personal issue. No doubt they have not allowed many people in on their secret, let alone a random person on the street.

Grace Given

If I were not an adoptive parent, might I be guilty of using some of the same terminology that is hurtful to me? Since I am an adoptive parent and cannot know this for sure, I must give grace to others who use insensitive words. After all, I recognize that when it comes to the many things outside my own realm of understanding, I can indeed demonstrate a lack of tact. I have only to look back on my exchange with Lori.

I choose to give people the benefit of the doubt by believing that most of the time they are unaware that their choice to question me—as well as the kinds of questions they ask—are hurtful.

When people tell me that they thought about adoption but then had children of their own, I try to put their comment in perspective. Maybe they did want to adopt but got pregnant before they could pursue that course of action. And maybe now the kids they have are all that they can handle, making adoption no longer an option for them.

People are curious about adoption, especially international adoption. That's a fact. It can be a positive thing to know that there are people who are interested, albeit abrasive in their attempts to get answers to their questions. Perhaps these are potential adoptive parents. The world needs more adoptions.

Handling It

Sometimes it feels that when it comes to the people I encounter who want to satisfy their curiosity, the ways in which they do it and the terminology they use in front of my children are all wrong. It makes my ability to give them grace difficult at best. And the hurt I feel for my kids is much worse than any irritation I may personally feel as a result of these people's questions. Yet hurt feelings must be set aside in order to fulfill my duty and my responsibility to my children. Our kids are keen to observe the ways in which we deal with others. For them we have to take the high road.

So when I am out and about and a stranger approaches me with "Do you have any of your own kids?" my first instinct is to protect my children and to assess any need for damage control. I read my kids' little faces for signs that they have heard the question and for their reaction, if any.

In most cases, though not all, I respond to people, even if what they said was inappropriate. While some may disagree with this approach and feel inclined to ignore hurtful parties, I think that there are good reasons to do otherwise.

Kids learn to deal with people from their parents. If a parent's response to strangers is always to ignore them, kids will imitate this behavior. If your kids have a natural curiosity about others and are sociable, as mine are, they just might ask you twenty questions about what it was the other person said, why you didn't answer them and so on. When kids are young, they can't differentiate between a comment or a question that warrants being ignored and one that might not. But there are times when responses can and should be given to people in order to teach kids this difference.

Modeling to children to ignore strangers who might say something a bit off promotes rudeness and translates to them that you can disregard strangers, when, for better or for worse, strangers constitute the vast majority of people we encounter every day.

For instance, children come into contact with a lot of kids at school. Curious, and often deficient in those little censors that tell us what may or may not be appropriate to say (which many adults never develop), these children have at times asked my kids adoption-related questions or made comments about adoption.

Rather than ignore these comments, my kids need to learn to be confident about who they are and to be able to respond. This will demonstrate to another child that my child is not vulnerable to the particular topic brought up and very well may prevent future comments or ugly questions.

Besides showing others that my children are self-assured, being able to respond to people helps to socialize my children through communication with others. It is often the child who seems withdrawn and quiet who gets picked on.

Of course, if questions or comments turn into taunts or verbal assaults, it is better for my children to ignore a bully and to bring matters to the attention of a teacher or the principal.

In general, answering tough questions also prevents children from the tendency of many to sweep unpleasantries under the proverbial rug. Failing to respond to others is a passive way of handling a personal affront. And as a parent with children who may receive more and different types of questions and comments than biological children will, I do not want my kids to take on other people's messes and hang onto them or stuff them. It is my job to demonstrate to them how to clean those up.

Teaching kids to stick up for themselves and to have ready answers, even to dumb questions, empowers them. Those answers provide foundational tools for effective communication with others. It also helps children to distinguish between people they should ignore because they pose a threat and those who are insensitive but simply curious.

Providing someone an appropriate, calm answer in front of my children defends my kids. Refusing to answer may make my children wonder if Mommy in fact thinks any less of them. They deserve to know that we think the right answer to the question "Do you have any of your own kids?" is yes. They can't process the implications of the question, nor can they process a silent response to it. It's our job to allay any fears or doubts our children may have by communicating with others.

"These are my children," is my standard answer. Then I disengage from the hurtful party.

Another helpful way of dealing with inappropriate questions stems from the view we hold of ourselves. I see myself as an adoptive parent who has in many ways carried and birthed my children. Of course, while we adoptive parents do not give birth to our children in the traditional sense, adoption is comparable to and often more difficult than pregnancy and birth in many ways.

I once watched a show called *Adoption Stories*. In the episode I saw, a woman's wait to adopt a son was to have taken only a few months but turned into almost two years. The woman's mother commented that the adoption process was similar to that of the gestational period of an elephant (elephants are pregnant with a single offspring for around two years).

China adoptions have become longer to process in recent years, and it hasn't been uncommon for couples who plan to adopt from this country to wait two to three years to see their adoptions through.

The truth is, since some couples who adopt from foreign countries, as well as some who pursue domestic adoptions, can wait more than three times the period of a pregnancy to see their child for the first time, they do, in fact, experience a type of pregnancy of their own.

Our love and anticipation for our child grows within our hearts. As pregnant women do, we "nest" as we prepare a nursery and buy baby items. We try out names for our child and imagine glimpses of the future when we will be together as a family. We are given baby showers. We also have our good days and our bad ones as do pregnant women. Sometimes we feel ready to explode, and we just want our baby in our arms. Other days we take advantage of our freedom until the baby comes. And instead of a proud display to family and friends of ultrasound pictures, we pull out our referral photo and share it.

Ready to "give birth," we may experience numerous bouts of false labor pains as one departure date turns into another and yet another after that. We worry about the health of our child through this extensive "pregnancy" and wonder if the late "birth" will pose serious risks to our baby's health. We think that the longer it takes to get him into our arms, the greater the threats to him that come from infection, a lack of proper nutrition and an unhealthy environment.

About to have her delivered into our arms, we are exhausted from having traveled halfway across the world. We may not check into a hospital, but we check into a hotel where, as in hospitals in this country, there are lots of people around us who speak in a language we don't understand. And like the woman who gives physical birth, we must relinquish control. We may not be assisted by doctors and nurses, but rather we have adoption coordinators, facilitators and translators all at work to calm our fears and move us along the process. As with birth, we must trust in the Lord that our child will be healthy and "normal."

When at long last we hold her, we cry tears of joy as do birth parents, and we count all her fingers and toes just to make sure they are all there.

After such a long and often arduous process, we have every reason to view our children as our own, as those we have in some way given birth to. Having only a split second to handle hurtful comments or questions that seem to challenge our parenthood, especially in front of our children, is an endless challenge. But discussion and acceptance of adoption is on the rise. As adoptive parents, we would like to see this continue.

It can also help if we remember that because we stopped to respond to someone, even if that person was a bit intrusive or offensive, we shared with him or her a truth or imparted some information. Perhaps God will use that moment to plant a seed in somebody else's heart whom He wants to lead on an adoption journey.

If our hearts are drawn to the godly ministry of adoption, then we should ask the Lord to place us in situations in which we may be used by Him to make a difference in this area. It should come as no surprise to us then, if we have prayerfully asked Him to do this, if we find ourselves facing unexpected and even difficult moments in which He wants to use us. These inconveniences and affronts may be opportunities for us to touch the lives of others in positive ways.

If more couples who wanted children would adopt, a radical

change in the lives of millions of abandoned children would sweep the globe. Not only would inappropriate and hurtful comments and questions directed toward adoptive parents and their children fade, but we could reduce children's hunger, neglect, depression, isolation, sickness and premature death.

The effect of millions of Christians choosing to adopt would bring huge numbers of children who might never otherwise be brought up with any faith into a situation in which they can be exposed to one through their parents. Two biblical mandates—to care for orphans (see James 1:27) and to spread the gospel (see Matt. 28:19)—could thus be accomplished through reaching out to one child.

Healing Questions

1. What are some of your thoughts on the terminology that refers to children as one's own rather than as adopted children?

2. Now that you have read this chapter, have any of your feelings changed as to the ways in which you may or may not respond to people who ask hurtful or intrusive questions?

3. How do you think that God can use you to plant seeds in others about adoption?

8

Do They Know They're Adopted?

Strangers have approached me in hushed tones and asked if my kids are aware of their adoptions. Friends I've known for years have sat at my kitchen table, when my children have been of school age and certainly old enough to be aware of their origins, and with lowered voices asked, "Do they know?" Even some of the teachers at Lucas' and Olivia's schools have inquired of me as to whether my children are aware that they are adopted.

All the raised eyebrows and shushed voices make it seem as though there has been a death in the family. These people sound worried that when my children find out about their adoptions, they will be crushed.

As I have pointed out, Lucas is from Vietnam and Olivia from China. My husband and I do not share their heritages. So, as incredible as it sounds, there are a number of people who must think that my children are blind or that we somehow managed to keep their adoptions a secret from them.

What Hurts

Part of me finds it almost humorous that others really do wonder if my school-aged Asian-born children who live with parents of European descent are in the dark about their adoptions.

Dad is well over six feet tall with dark blond hair and hazel eyes. Mom has curly hair and definitely does not possess the petite frame of an Asian woman. How could their adoptions be a secret to Lucas and Olivia?

Another part of me, though, finds the question objectionable. When my kids were small enough to sit in a grocery cart and a complete stranger would come within an inch of my ear to whisper this question in a serious, low tone of voice, it threatened my children. It threatened me too, for that matter.

As I experienced yet another violation of a boundary that no stranger is entitled to cross, no doubt my children watched my body tense in both fear and disgust. Kids are sharp; they pick up on our body language; and what these situations translated into for my kids was potential danger for me and maybe for them too.

Plus, this stranger had given my children a solemn stare as he asked me the question. No one has the right to step almost on top of a kid's mother or father while he or she shoots the child a stony gaze. Only crazy people do that, right?

Absolutely the worst aspect of this scenario is when my children actually hear the question asked. It's both insensitive and degrading for someone to draw attention to a family because its members don't look like you and to demand personal information.

And what if, for some reason, my children did not know? How terrible would it be for a young child to find out from a complete stranger that he or she is adopted!

This question is such an assault to a child's developing identity. It is also rude and demonstrates a total disregard for the fact that the children are present and have ears that hear and minds that seek to understand why the question is being asked in the first place. I have worried that my kids can't help but think that others notice that they are "different" and that they stand out in public. Do they wonder if they appear weird and somehow not normal when they are with my husband and me?

Adoptive parents can become weary of all the reminders from others that they are an adoptive family. We don't want these interjections into our lives that can make our children feel different or abnormal or that they are oddities.

When a neighbor asks me whether or not my kids know they are adopted over a cup of coffee and while my kids aren't present, I'm not quite as offended as I would be if the children were there. However, it does bother me to hear my neighbor assume that such a secret might be kept from Lucas and Olivia. The implication in her question is that I don't bother to talk to my kids about where they have come from or about why we don't look related until the children come to me and ask. Or maybe she thinks my children will spend the rest of their lives not noticing our physical differences. If people who ask this question thought about it, they would realize that not speaking to my adopted children about their adoptions or heritages, especially since they are foreign-born, could even be irresponsible or unloving. Every child deserves to know the truth as soon as possible.

Also, friends who ask this fail to take into account the fact that Lucas had almost reached four years of age when we adopted his sister, so he was old enough to remember Olivia's adoption. He insisted on accompanying us to China before my husband and I had decided whether or not we would take him, and he knew full well why we were going there.

Furthermore, wouldn't people expect that we would have mementos, memorabilia, photo albums and DVDs from our trips to Vietnam and China? Do they think that we would hide all this from our children?

Grace Given

I'll admit that at times when people have asked me if my children know that they are adopted, I have stared at them as if they have just landed from another planet. But then I remember that it is important to give them grace.

I can say that I have met families created through international adoption in which the parents have chosen not to share with their children the truth that they are adopted. Of course, in these cases the parents and children look similar to each other, or at least a lot more alike than my children resemble my husband and me. Perhaps some of those hush-toned visitors to my table and my grocery cart know these people too.

While far more children today know that they are adopted than adopted children did years ago, views on adoption being a hush-hush subject still exist.

Some people only know what they have heard or been told by someone else about adoption. The information they have received may be untrue and have caused them to believe that adoption should not be discussed with children or that children will be hurt if they find out the truth.

Years ago our society's widely held view on adoption was that a child should not know, for various reasons, that he or she had been adopted. Many parents just did not want to talk about it with their child. For one thing, any discussion might have caused an adoptive parent to relive his or her anguish and shame of infertility, or perhaps it would have threatened the stability of the happy home the parent had worked hard to create. In addition, adoptive parents worried that if there happened to be biological children living in the household as well, the adopted child might feel out of place or loved less than the others.

Besides these issues, there is sometimes a threat to family relationships when adopted children search for their birth parents or when biological parents search for their kids.

I read of a woman who had a grown adopted son. This young man was searched for and found by his birth mother, who had not seen him since he had been born. The adoptive mother was ambivalent about her son meeting his biological parent. While she wanted him to have some of his lifelong questions answered, she couldn't help but feel that she was at risk of losing him. The conflict she felt was only compounded by the fact that her two older children had passed away.

Some adoptive parents cannot bear the thought that they might face rejection by their children. A common fear is that the adopted child will reconnect with a biological family and that he or she might choose that one over the adoptive one, then move away and lose touch with the parents who have loved and cared for him or her over the years.

Others feel quite protective too; they worry that their adoptive children may suffer a second abandonment filled with pain and disappointment if their birth parents do not meet their expectations.

While these issues are more closely tied to domestic adoption, this is all that many people understand about adoption in general. But with the world getting smaller, there are even cases of birth parents reaching out across the globe to try and make contact with internationally adopted children, although these cases are rare.

I choose to give people the benefit of the doubt, even though it seems obvious to me that my children must know that I did not give birth to them. I realize that we all fumble our way through situations outside our own experience.

Handling It

I confess that the flesh part of me has wanted at times to make some who have asked me this question feel stupid. I have struggled not to say, "Do they know they're adopted? Why no! We thought we'd keep it a secret since they look so much like my husband and me!"

And I've quelled the urge to shout at that stranger whom my kids have overheard with a "Gee thanks, now they know!"

However, rather than resort to sarcasm with the end result being a comment that you don't want your kids to hear, we have to remove ourselves and our children from an offensive person. "Stay away a fool, for you won't find knowledge on their lips." (Prov. 14:7 NIV). When it comes to a stranger asking this question in front of our kids, this command qualifies. That's because besides being a bit ludicrous, the question is an intrusive one that does not serve any purpose. Unlike a friend or family member who asks us in private because they want to know if they should avoid mentioning adoption around our children, a stranger who asks is being nosy and self-serving.

While I don't mind answering many kinds of questions related to adoption, at times there just has to be a line drawn to protect my children and to let others know that they have overstepped boundaries at the expense of my kids. These curiosity seekers also need to know that we do not give permission to just anyone to approach us with any and every personal inquiry.

When my neighbor asked me if my kids knew of their adoptions, part of me wanted to ask her to go and look for a mirror in our home. Instead, though, I took the time to help her understand how my children know that they are adopted.

I explained to her that parents who internationally adopt must begin to tell their children their adoption stories early on. This way truth never turns into a secret or gets shoved under a rug. Secrets, for the most part, end up uncovered. And if they are locked away, then the longer it takes to reveal them, the more of a shock they tend to create when exposed, since they are difficult to accept and to deal with. Secrets, by the very nature of their concealment, infer that there is something negative and unacceptable about what is being hidden. Adoption is none of that.

On the other hand, a child's adoption should not be some great, big revelation that permeates his or her every waking moment. Adoptive parents must gauge their children's interest in and sensitivity to their birth heritage and the way they became part of the family—I will discuss this at greater length later in this book. If we consider adoption a unique and special aspect of our children that has blessed us, then our children accept it as another of the qualities that make them who they are.

Besides this, from the time that John and I brought our children home, we both acknowledged and celebrated aspects of their native cultures and holidays. We also bought keepsakes and presents from our kids' native countries, which we give to them on the anniversaries of their adoptions—what we call their "Gotcha Day."

As parents, we often have to weigh a situation that is hurtful to our children, balancing between being their protector and not creating a negative situation. In other words, we don't want to turn an unpleasant situation volatile by yelling or cursing or, heaven forbid, shoving someone who is breathing a rather hurtful, intrusive question down our necks. We don't want to abuse people who are ignorant or insensitive.

In some instances I have had but a split second to decide whether I will or will not respond to someone's hurtful comment. These are times when I launch my "rocket prayers." These are on-the-spot appeals to the Lord for good judgment and wise choices. No prayer is too sudden for His attention.

Sometimes God tells me to walk away. But other times He provides the opportunity for me to right a wrong. This may take the form of sharing truth where a false assumption or erroneous idea exists. And that can be the most rewarding outcome of these unpleasant moments.

Healing Questions

1. Have you ever struggled with intrusive questions or comments about your adopted child?

2. What are some of the ways you have handled such comments?

3. Has a hurtful comment or question about adoption ever provided you with an opportunity to educate someone about adoption? How do you think it could?

9

Are They, You Know, Normal?

At long last I caught a glimpse of her from across the room where we and eleven other couples waited with bated breath to receive our babies. A pale-green ski coat and matching pants swallowed her up as she sat on a caretaker's lap. It was over sixty degrees outside. At least we would get clothing with her, unlike when we had picked up our son in Vietnam three years earlier.

Olivia sat motionless. Shiny, straight black hair parted to the side gave me a good look at her fair-skinned, petite face that was filled with what appeared to be anxiety and sadness.

Finally my husband and I were called to the center of the room and handed our bulky blessing. I blinked back tears of joy as I got a good look at her. Olivia began to wail, which didn't surprise me. But after her initial outburst she just withdrew, shrinking into a place where I could not reach her. She did not make eye contact. She didn't smile. She didn't make any sounds. She wouldn't eat or drink. The preliminary sadness I had seen on her beautiful face spread to the rest of her body, which at thirteen months old did not crawl or walk or grab at toys.

When I placed Olivia in a baby carrier against my body in an effort to try and bond with her, she hung there like a wet dishrag.

I had not even for a moment anticipated that I would receive an unresponsive baby who was filled with despair.

In fact, my disturbing reality in China ran counter to any and every concept I had of what a baby is and does. Olivia didn't seem normal to me.

With each dismal hour that ticked by, my heart struggled to accept this little girl. I glumly watched the other babies in our group of twelve families toddle or run around in the hotel restaurant where we all gathered for meals. Those who sat in strollers or high chairs crammed fistfuls of Cheerios and other foods into their mouths with gusto. They squeezed new siblings' faces and pulled napkins off tables. All the while, my beautiful child—the prettiest in the group, really—sat motionless with no expression on her face at all.

During Olivia's first bath in the hotel, she curled forward, a protruding bone-after-bone outline of her spine visible. Aghast, I watched as she lowered her face into the couple of inches of water in the tub and left it there! Panicked, I lifted her head out of the water. I literally had to hold her head up while finishing her bath so she wouldn't drown. Tears rolled down my cheeks. She turned into a blurred speck in a large tub.

As I wept and rushed through Olivia's bath, my mind wandered back to my son Lucas' first bath three years earlier in Vietnam. He had made John and me smile and laugh as we had watched him kick his legs and grab at plastic tub toys in frantic excitement. He had giggled and squealed with such delight.

My heart ached for Olivia those first few days, but it was near breaking for me too. A practically catatonic baby who rejects the love for her that wants to burst from a mother's heart grinds one down.

Will she never love me? I wondered. *Will she ever be able to bond with me? Have I not prayed enough for her? What am I doing wrong?* I felt as if I was Olivia's worst nightmare come true. My mother, who had joined us for the trip, reassured me that Olivia would be just fine in time.

Just when I thought what little there was to my baby would wither away and die if she didn't eat or drink, Mom discovered that Olivia liked watermelon. Though it was high in sugar, I knew it would help prevent dehydration. At every meal Mom hunted some down, cut it into tiny pieces and with great patience hand-fed it to her.

By only our second night in China, I asked my mother to babysit. My husband and I went to the hotel lounge.

"Gee, it's nice to have your mother along to help out," John said with a smile. "I'm glad we're getting some alone time," he said while holding my hand.

"Uh-huh," I murmured. I forced myself to return his smile. More than enjoying time alone with my husband, I felt glad for a reprieve from our sad baby.

The next morning Mom greeted us and delivered her verdict that based on her time with Olivia the evening before, there existed a fiery little temper underneath the baby's flat affect. I remained unconvinced, and by now, the third day, I could take Olivia's demeanor no longer. I was positive that our new baby suffered from some sort of neurological deficit. Maybe God had placed her in our arms so that we would be able to initiate a process whereby she could get much needed medical help. But adopt her? I wasn't so sure anymore.

At breakfast I lifted her limp frame from her high chair and marched over to our adoption coordinator.

"There's something wrong with her!" I frightened myself by the frantic sound of my voice.

Our coordinator studied Olivia. She spoke to her in her native Chinese and playfully shook her arms and hands. She held her and looked into her eyes. Olivia's response during this whole time seemed below minimal.

"See?" I wailed. "I'm concerned there's some sort of neurological impair—" Our coordinator, Ellen, cut me off.

"There's nothing wrong with this baby," she informed me.

Stunned, I stood there. How could she know that in the space of about one minute and without having any kind of medical degree? I waited for an explanation.

"She's just sad," she explained. "Play with her a lot."

Oh, how I wanted to believe her! Yet I was skeptical. At the same time, everyone else too seemed to think that Olivia was OK.

Mom thought that she was fine and fiery. Ellen said that she was sad but normal. Even my husband didn't seem too concerned with what I viewed as signs of a disturbed child.

Over the next couple of days, Olivia seemed to warm up to one person: her big brother Lucas. If ever there was a child to warm up to, with his exuberant, outgoing personality and thirst for fun, it would be Lucas. I actually saw Olivia smile a little as she and Lucas sat on the bed together one afternoon, hands clasped.

John found a way to cheer her too. While we were out sightseeing and shopping for souvenirs, he took her from the baby carrier in which I carried her everywhere. As he held her, he realized that her tiny bottom fit perfectly in the palm of his large hand. With a tight grip on the back of her tights, he extended his arm from his six-foot, two-and-a-half-inch frame and held her out in front of him as we walked.

The shroud of sadness and apathy that had enveloped her started to lift. She craned her little chicken-like neck and looked around, content and unafraid!

Shocked but also relieved, I watched her, feeling gratitude and a little guilt. While I had stuffed her tightly into a carrier, desperate for mother/daughter bonding, she had wanted her freedom. My heart also felt a sting of jealousy and rejection. Everyone but me had gotten through to Olivia somehow!

On our fifth and final day in Hunan Province, where Olivia had been born, our entourage of adoptive families formed a line at the airport. More than ready, we were about to board a plane for the city of Guangzhou in order to finalize our adoptions. With my daughter back in the baby carrier for practical reasons, I helped carry luggage and kept track of my son's busy steps. There Olivia hung, face in my chest lest her beautiful countenance be bumped by travelers or suitcases, the sad baby who didn't seem to want me for a mother.

I stood in silence, impatient for our boarding passes to be issued. Yet my heart's cry was loud.

"How long can I go on like this, Lord?" I prayed.

Then I looked down at this precious baby that the Lord had, for reasons only He knew, chosen me to mother. Olivia lifted her head and looked up at me, directly into my eyes for the first time! I stared at her in disbelief. She continued to meet my gaze when, to my utter amazement, her tiny, soft voice that I had not yet heard floated up to me.

"Mama," she said.

"She called me Mama!" I shouted to my family.

Lucas, John and my mother all surrounded Olivia and me. We laughed, cried, hugged and made a spectacle of ourselves in a Chinese airport.

Everyone had been right. My baby was going to be fine.

Just what is normal for the newly adopted child? Is it the absence of any shred of physical or mental illness? Is it being developmentally on target? Emotionally well adjusted? Fat and happy?

What Hurts

Well before John and I had boarded planes to adopt babies from Vietnam and China, family and friends had expressed worries that we had been duped into lifetime commitments to sick or otherwise "abnormal" orphans. They told us that they feared we were about to enter into a blind trust with what they felt was the crooked world of adoption out to take a lot of our money and then fail to produce a baby or else to rid some country of a "burdensome" human being.

"You're being scammed!" some declared.

"You can't trust the agency to give you a healthy child," others commented.

"I've seen the picture of your son," a few said, "and he doesn't look normal."

"Why's his head so flat?"

"Why can't she sit up?"

"A lot of the babies in this video look sick."

"He could have AIDS."

We adoptive parents, just as do those who give birth, hope and pray for a healthy child. Even so, John and I knew that our babies might be handed to us sick with colds or infections. They would likely require better nutrition than they had previously had. And they could well have skin conditions, scabies or anemia. A strong possibility existed that they would have developmental delays due to lack of physical stimulation. And, of course, we anticipated some transitional difficulties as our children left the only lives they had known and grew to trust us.

All of us who embark on an adoption journey are aware of the potential missing pieces in the full picture of our children's health. We take unknowns into consideration, pray about them and have faith that our children will be okay. In light of these certain "unknowns" and all the other stress already associated with any adoption procedure, it hurts when people confront us about everything that may possibly go wrong.

Many of the comments that John and I were bombarded with about our upcoming adoptions frustrated and alarmed us. Against my will, my mind sometimes wandered to frightening places. I felt blamed in advance for making what I knew might be a risky decision.

Grace Given

While it's difficult to listen to people worry about how our adoptions can go wrong, I can give them grace based on my experience. It is true too that people, me included, have heard of some serious, heartbreaking adoption cases.

Many of us are aware of people whose babies at first seemed normal at adoption only to later be given diagnoses of fetal alcohol syndrome or attachment disorders. Sometimes these problems can be devastating and test parents beyond their abilities to bond with and care for their children.

And many of us have probably heard of deplorable conditions for orphans who live in certain countries. Irreparable physical and emotional harm can be done to these children through the abuse and neglect they suffer. Because of all the media coverage of these kinds of situations, it's possible for many to assume that international adoption equals getting compromised children.

When people make assumptions or hold preconceived notions on adoption, there may be a speck of truth in what they believe. Bad things can happen. People may take advantage of us. And an adopted child is a great unknown in terms of the mixed bag of experience and genetics he or she carries into our lives. This is precisely why giving grace is so important. There's an iota of verity in the potential that something could be "wrong" with an adopted child. It's just that putting this fact to an adoptive parent in an insensitive or hysterical fashion is hurtful.

It's important to give ourselves grace for our own worries too as we prepare for our adoption journeys.

We already have such an emotional investment in a faraway little stranger; we can't help but concern ourselves with that little one. We wonder what he may be doing at any given moment. We hope that she is warm, well-fed and held often enough. We think about his caretakers and hope that they are qualified and interested enough in their important jobs. We pray all the time for our babies.

And we lack so much information. Often we don't have a clue as to the health of our children's biological parents. We don't know if their birth mothers received any kind of prenatal care. We don't have any idea whether or not our babies were preterm or experienced difficult births.

What might be their genetic predispositions? This unanswerable question can be one of the most worrisome to adoptive parents. I know that I found my mind going to some pretty dark places during our wait for our children. The endless delays in the adoption process can wear us down and leave us vulnerable to all sorts of frantic thinking.

Handling It

Hurtful comments that people make about our adoptions can be sudden. Without warning and certainly without our permission, these can be dumped on us. It's sort of like having the mail carrier appear on your curb on a Sunday and hit you over the head with a sack of junk mail. There you were, enjoying a day of rest, when wham! You're hit over the head with a mess to sort through and clean up.

It's important, especially if people make comments in front of your children, to let others know that it's not acceptable for them to ask if your kids are "normal," implying that they are flawed or defective, simply because they are adopted. I have uttered a loud and forceful "They're more normal than most!" when I have been asked this question in front of Lucas and Olivia so that there would be no doubt in my children's minds that they are indeed normal. Then I have removed myself from the inquisitive person in order to protect my children.

This isn't to say that I won't speak with someone who in private asks about the initial health of my children. As an adoption advocate, it is my privilege to provide truthful information to those who genuinely are concerned about the potential risks of adoption. I tell such people that despite cases of adopted children who have grave disorders or conditions, these are usually few and far between. As is common with media coverage, we're bombarded with extremes, since adopted children who blossom and flourish aren't all that newsworthy.

It's helpful to remember that any child, whether he or she is adopted, fostered, biological or part of a stepfamily, represents a parent's commitment to a lifetime of unknowns.

It's up to us adoptive parents to carefully examine the "seeds" handed to us by others. We have to ask ourselves and the Lord, are these weeds that will create a jungle and hinder our adoption paths? Or shall we instead plant God's seeds and see that, according to the book of Ecclesiastes, He makes everything beautiful in its own time?

If we can't step out in faith, we might not be ready for adoption.

As for Olivia, what appeared to me an abnormality in her was actually something that was able to be viewed in a positive light. Her behavior those first few rocky days with us meant that she had bonded well with her former caretakers. It demonstrated that she was capable of bonding and that she would bond again.

And that she has.

Healing Questions

1. Have you ever been discouraged by others about your adoption plan because you might receive a less-than-perfect child? How did you handle this?

2. Did you worry that you might be adopting a child who could present issues or concerns to you? If so, were you able to overcome your worries? How?

3. In what ways has your child blessed your life?

10

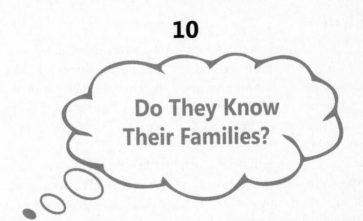

Do They Know Their Families?

Let's look for some blue sneakers," I said to then-four-year-old Olivia. Seven-year-old Lucas sat on a bench, arms folded, anxious for the shoe-shopping excursion to come to an end.

I sat my daughter down next to her brother while the salesgirl went to get Olivia's size in the pale-blue shoes that she had picked out.

A man sidled up to us while his child picked out some shoelaces at the counter. He smiled down at my two. My mommy antennae were raised by the way he just stood there and stared and smiled for what seemed an inordinate amount of time.

"Cute kids," he said at last.

"Thank you," I replied.

"Do they know their families?" he wanted to know.

I felt my mouth drop open as I grabbed both of my kids' hands, jumped up and headed straight for the back room. I almost smacked into the poor salesgirl who teetered backward with three or four boxes of shoes clutched to her chest.

"I'm so sorry," I apologized, helping to steady the boxes in her arms. "We're kind of in a rush."

"Oh, *I'm* sorry," she said. "We're out of the blue ones, but I brought a bunch of others for her to try on."

To my relief the guy and his son were gone when we walked back into the main part of the store.

What Hurts

It shouldn't take a person more than a second to realize that if he or she asks me if my kids know their family, what the person is really wondering is if my children know their mother—who obviously happens to be with them. It's so wrong. I'm not surprised that we found this guy where we did. It seems that he likes the taste of shoe leather.

To me, the situation we experienced that day felt equivalent to having an armed lunatic show up on the scene. This man essentially crashed through my kids' everyday world while they were on an outing with Mom and waved a gun over them as he shouted, "You don't belong with her! Where are your real parents?"

However, I could not scream "Security!" because this man did not terrorize my children with a gun or ski mask. He just happened to be some shopper in khakis and a blazer. *A* for presentation—*F* minus for performance.

Why would anyone ask children if they know their families when they are out with their mother? It implies to them that they are in the wrong place with the wrong person. Why wouldn't someone give half a thought about how much damage such a comment can do to an innocent, vulnerable child's sense of identity and security?

I'd like to see "Khaki Pants and Blazer" walk up to another parent who has children who look like her and ask her, "Do they know their grandmother?" or, "What can you tell me about their ancestors?" or, "Are these kids adopted, or are they really yours?"

But this kind of thing just doesn't happen—unless, of course, Khaki Pants is plain crazy. And in truth, I would not want to see biological families put through this. It's just that an adoptive parent can get frustrated with these kinds of in-your-face, inappropriate questions and comments that can hurt our kids.

If people think that we have a foreign-born child and want to know if our kids know their birth families, perhaps they should learn a few things first.

There is a huge difference between domestic and international adoption in terms of the anonymity of the biological parents and the information available about them. We often know little about an international child's pre-abandonment history, genetic makeup and health.

For some couples, including my husband and me, it was this anonymity that drew us more toward international adoption than to domestic adoption or foster care, even though it creates potential risks and uncertainties about the child. A child placed in an orphanage overseas is unlikely to have a birth parent pop up later on and want to reunite with him or her. And the fact that in foreign countries the ties are more fully severed between birth parent and child made us think that international adoption gave a baby the most likely possibility of getting a chance to experience parenting outside an orphanage setting.

Lucas was born in a hospital and named by his biological mother, and his adoption by us is a matter of public record. Because of this, it is possible for his birth parents to find out what happened to him. But there are reasons that it would be more plausible for them not to contact us.

For one thing, the geographical distance between Vietnam and the United States creates a great barrier. To phone or travel overseas can be prohibitive for a couple that may not have the means.

For another, to give birth out of wedlock, as Lucas' biological mother did, is considered shameful in many countries. This shame contributes to women abandoning their children and perhaps putting them out of their mind—insofar as that is possible. If the birth parents have married other people and moved on with their lives, a previously conceived child whom they had given up would not even be mentioned to a spouse or family members.

In cases of anonymous abandonment in which a child may not have been born in a hospital or a medical facility and has had his or her name changed, a successful search for the biological child or later for the mother by the child is highly unlikely.

This was my daughter's situation. Left outside the gates of an orphanage, her age was approximated by the orphanage staff, who also gave her a name. This is quite common in China.

This anonymity with regard to biological ancestry can be a double-edged sword for adoptive families. While we are confident that no one will appear to try and reclaim our children, we feel moments of sadness for both our children and for their birth parents over the finality of their separation.

While "with God all things are possible" (Matt. 19:26), and He could orchestrate a reunion between my kids and their biological parents that would awe us by His power to do anything He chooses, it appears that this has not been His intention, based on our experience over these past several years.

My children probably won't be able to meet the people who brought them into the world and ask them the question every adoptee wonders: "Why?"

They won't know if they have any biological siblings or what their ancestors may have experienced or accomplished. They won't be able to see the only faces that reflect their own look back at them. I sometimes wonder—although at their young ages my children have never expressed a desire to know their birth parents—if when they get older, the inability to have their questions answered will bother them.

But even more so, at least for now, is the sadness I sometimes feel for my children's birth parents. In particular I think about their birth mothers and how the abandonment of their babies has affected their lives. I know that giving up these children must have caused them pain and grief.

I wish they could know the amazing son and daughter they have blessed us with! As each of my children has grown each year, especially around their birthdays, I have imagined what their birth parents would think of them. I would love for them to know how beautiful, smart, funny and special they are.

If either of my children's birth parents ever tried to contact us, I would want them to experience a relationship with their biological son or daughter. I would want to honor the people who gave us so much blessing through their pain and loss.

Yet another perspective on international adoption is that the lack of ties with birth parents results in a more stable and consistent upbringing for the children. Unlike that of domestic adoption or foster care, we never have to deal with the complexities of incorporating another family into our own. There are no holidays spent at multiple homes or long-distance drives for visitations between our children and their biological families. We won't have children torn between two sets of parents and siblings, bouncing back and forth and mourning time away from relatives. They won't have to experience the potential for two types of discipline, different worldviews or conflicts in cultural beliefs or faiths.

Grace Given

We live in an age in which more birth parents are choosing "open adoptions," whereby adoptive parents and their child continue with various forms of contact and/or relationship with the child's biological parent or parents. In some scenarios the birth parents may have regular visitations. In others there may be no contact, but pictures may be sent to the birth parents on a regular basis. These details depend on how the involved parties reach an agreement as to what is best for everyone involved.

Sometimes birth parents may want to have regular visits with their biological children but then taper off these meetings. They may move far away, "move on" with their lives or find the original agreement too emotionally draining or painful.

Today's foster-care system works harder to cultivate more contact between children who are in the system and their parents. The goal to reunify foster children with their birth parents has increased, except in cases, of course, in which the child would come to harm if this were done.

Perhaps the ways in which family has been redefined and living situations for adoptive and fostered children have changed causes people to wonder if my Asian-born children know their birth families. Perhaps they think that my kids are American-born foster kids or adopted kids.

Due in large part to the existence of the Internet, the world has gotten smaller. The ability to contact people halfway across the globe with the click of a mouse just might perpetuate the notion that adoptive parents and their children have instant access to the kids' foreign birth parents. For these reasons I give people who think my children know their families grace.

Grace is necessary also because as of late, there are more cases of foreign birth parents or relatives who meet a child's new adoptive parents. I have watched and read about some of these incidents in which poverty or illness has caused families to give up children. When the children are adopted by overseas couples, the biological parents or siblings or even extended family often visit the orphanage or facility where the child has been living to say goodbye to him or her. In these cases it is possible for the adopted children to receive pictures or addresses or other personal information from their biological families.

I realize too that humans can be quite curious by nature and that they often overstep boundaries in order to satisfy their need to know things. I offer grace to people who live in a society that no longer seems to keep any of its business to itself. Still, all these realizations have not prevented me from feeling righteous anger for being asked difficult questions in front of my children.

Handling It

Although I know that I am justified in my anger when another's insensitive curiosity has a negative impact on my children, the wise response is for me not to unleash that anger on the offender.

God understands our anger. He Himself gets angry over sin, injustice and our disobedience. Though we are allowed to get angry, He instructs us, "Be angry and do not sin" (Eph. 4:26).

If we scream at an offensive stranger, or worse, then we sin— even though there are times when we may want to react this way. Not only this, but when we put our children in an emotionally disturbing situation, we sin against them as well. We do more than frighten them; we leave indelible impressions on their fragile psyches that they must carry with them always.

It is important, too, that we be aware that in situations of conflict, violence may never be far off.

Even if we live in a good neighborhood, we are not guaranteed freedom from trouble. Irrational and angry actions can cross socioeconomic boundaries. Any unpleasant interaction can escalate into assault or worse when we haven't a clue as to who we might be dealing with or how close to the edge that person might be. In particular, this is true when we encounter others dealing with stressors in their lives such as racial disharmony, economic hardship or great personal challenges. They carry with them a heightened sense of injustice and tension.

But still we must act. If another's hurtful words or deeds affect us, we are required to deal with their behavior. We must choose whether we will implement action through our physical bodies— such as I did that day in the shoe store by walking away—or through our words, thoughts, prayers or a combination of these. And we must do it without sinning.

Even with all this to consider over the space of only seconds, we must take into account that God's Word further instructs us not to "repay evil for evil . . . but...a blessing" (1 Pet. 3:9).

If you've gotten the impression that we are to protect our children, keep a cool head and resist the very real temptation to strike out in anger toward another's words and then to repay our offender with kindness, then you've understood me correctly. All this sometimes requires more than action—it necessitates a monumental effort. I confess that many times I have to force myself to act and speak with kindness toward people whom I don't feel deserve such, regarding adoption issues or otherwise.

It's oh, so hard to give that nasty neighbor a cheerful hello when we see him or her out on the block.

And my feet feel as if they are lead weights when I drag myself to the store to purchase a birthday gift for someone who never remembers me on my birthday nor ever thanks me for a gift.

I wrestle with myself before I give a Christmas tip to the mailman who never bothers to turn the flag down after he picks up our outgoing mail or to the garbagemen who scatter my trash bins all over the block a couple times a week, sometimes mysteriously misplacing the lids.

Now these actions may not be "evil" that I repay with kindness, but left to grow roots of bitterness and resentment, these kinds of hurts can build to the point at which they seem intentional and malicious. That is why little things can become big ones and why people divorce because a spouse leaves the cap off the toothpaste tube. (OK, there are no statistics to verify that, but you get the idea.)

God wants us to protect our children, but He never expects us to be doormats. We are not required to allow ourselves to be violated.

I protect my children and myself with constant practice. I resist my impulses, keep my cool and remove myself and my kids from harmful situations. But I can also speak truth and answer people's ridiculous questions. I could have told Khaki Pants, "Of course they know their family. I'm right here with them, and my husband sees them every night when he comes home from work." That answer may have caused him to walk away, and as he headed off in another direction, I might have asked God to help me forgive him. But I chose not to respond to this particular guy, as there just happened to be something about him that made me want to flee with my kids.

We can't prevent ourselves from ever being hurt. And it can be even more painful when our child is the one who suffers from a question we are asked in front of him or her. But the sooner we make the conscious effort to forgive in these situations, the better.

The longer we practice this trying lesson, with God's help it becomes a bit easier.

Healing Questions

1. How difficult has it been for you to implement Ephesians 4:26 ("Be angry and do not sin") in your life?

2. What do you think about the idea that when others' stinging words affect us, we are required to deal with them?

3. Do you think it's possible to repay evil with blessing as instructed in First Peter 3:9? How?

11

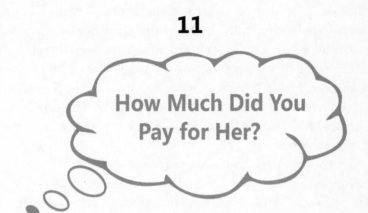

How Much Did You Pay for Her?

While stuffing green beans into a plastic bag at my local supermarket one morning, I almost bumped into a burly stranger. I gazed up past his red plaid shirt, burgundy jacket and thick moustache. He looked me in the eye as he gestured abruptly with his head in the direction of my two children who sat in a shopping cart. I glanced at my then four- and two-year-olds to see whether they had stolen fruit or stood up in the wagon. But Lucas and Olivia just sat there with serene expressions, munching the cookies I'd bought them as a treat.

"How much did you pay?" he wanted to know.

I glanced into my cart. "You mean for the cookies?" I asked.

"No, for her," he said, pointing to my daughter.

From the beginning of our adoption journey, my husband and I had seen God's hand in the receiving of our children. Naïve first-time homeowners at the time we decided to pursue adoption, my husband and I didn't realize that we were in over our heads with the house we had just purchased. Though John had a decent job at the time, we had no savings, and I supplemented his income with paltry earnings from a part-time waitressing job. We didn't exactly have the funds for an expensive adoption.

After much frustration and discouragement on the domestic front, we decided to go the international adoption route. One of the first things required of us for adopting a foreign-born child was to file an application with the Department of Immigration and Naturalization Services. We didn't even have the $180 it cost to do this. But while we were completing the application, John received an unexpected request from a former colleague asking if he could purchase John's old scuba-diving equipment. The only stipulation was that we pay the shipping costs. The proceeds after we sent him the equipment? Exactly $180.

Greatly encouraged by God's provision, we moved forward in the adoption process and scheduled our home study—a bigger leap of faith that would cost us $800. Before a social worker ever arrived at our house to approve its suitability for a child, John received an unanticipated $700 bonus from work. We praised and thanked God. But when that same week a friend of mine sent us a $100 check to help with our adoption costs, we were humbled and sure that God was paving the way for us to become parents.

Soon we received the referral for our baby boy in Vietnam. When I looked at the picture that our adoption facilitator emailed us on that sun-drenched June morning and saw a two-month-old baby boy, his spiky hair pointed every which way like a baby duck's and his angel lips that pouted over two chins, all in the space of an instant my heart surged and declared, "Mine!" For a week I leafed through pages of a baby-name book and felt that I understood, finally, what it means to be an expectant mom. We chose the name Lucas for our new son, which means "bringer of light."

On the eighth night of my newfound joy, however, as I climbed into bed next to John, I knew in an instant that something was wrong.

"I lost my job today," he blurted.

Uncontrollable sobs erupted from the bottom of my heart. The thought of losing my son, as alive and real and as much mine as if he were kicking inside of me, filled me with anguish. I refused to believe that God would show us His provision this far and then rip it all away. But another part of me thought that perhaps I'd been wrong after all and that this particular baby belonged to someone else. Maybe our house too really belonged to another family who could afford to pay the mortgage.

My expectation was that those close to me would console me in my terrible grief and fear. Yet my sister, a wiser and more mature Christian than I, told me not to throw in the proverbial towel. And our pastor urged John and I not to allow our lack of finances to make a decision for us as to whether or not we were meant to have this baby boy. He told us that God would make a way. I felt some encouragement, but I honestly did not see how the now-grim picture of our lives could change.

But God sees the bigger picture.

Another call came just days after John lost his job. This time a friend asked us if we wouldn't mind putting up a friend of hers in our spare bedroom. Apparently this woman had been transferred to our area for her job.

I was reluctant to say yes. I wanted to help, but I have to admit that I wasn't much in the mood to deal with a houseguest. But my friend gently persisted. She said it would only be for a couple of weeks and that our housemate would gladly pay us for our trouble. Practicality trumped my lack of desire to allow an outsider into this wretched time of our lives, and I said yes. Even if we were paid just a little bit, it would be a little bit more than nothing.

Jenna wasn't what I had expected at all. She left our house each morning before sunrise. She returned late at night. She even had her showers at her office's gym facility every day after her workout. She never ate a morsel of our food, as she was on a strict diet.

After her first week with us, she sat down at our kitchen table one evening to write us a check. I told her that we couldn't possibly accept any money from her. But she insisted and told us that she was giving us her company's hotel allowance.

"But instead of requiring that I stay at a hotel," she explained, "my employer lets me stay at a house so that I can have access to a kitchen for my diet and my liquid vitamins. Plus," she added, "I like to help people who can use the money."

My husband and I took the check. We stared at each other, openmouthed, after we glanced at the amount. Her company allotment could have paid for a five-star hotel!

Jenna's two-week assignment was extended, one week at a time, until the summer ended. Through her God brought us from nearly penniless to solvent.

John went on job interviews, while I baby-proofed the house and prepared the nursery. And while we had been honest with our adoption agency about John's job loss, contrary to my worries, the agency did not cancel our adoption. In fact, our facilitator shared her confidence with us that my husband would soon have another job.

Before Jenna left our home at the end of August, God provided John with a good job that paid 33 percent more than he had made at his previous job. That increase was necessary, we would soon discover, with a baby to support and all the unanticipated expenses that come along with homeownership.

I found myself on a roller coaster of joy and disappointment as our travel plans to bring Lucas home were scheduled, then cancelled, some seven times. John was eager to begin his new job and asked if he might start on September 11, 2001. His new boss told him to just relax and wait until we returned from Vietnam.

On the morning of the day that my husband had requested to be at his new job, I woke up and, turning on the news, realized that the world had turned upside down. The World Trade Towers sank into smoking heaps of rubble as our nation found itself blindsided by terrorism. John's new place of employment was located directly next to the towers and was heavily damaged. An employee of his new firm perished in the building.

After that, we were told by our adoption agency that the Vietnamese government refused to release any babies to couples living close to New York City. That older, wiser sister of mine now helped me to realize that our battle to become Lucas' parents wasn't a physical one but rather the spiritual kind in which we had to fall to our knees, believing that God would see our journey to fruition. After all, He'd brought us through so much in specific and amazing ways to get us to the brink of becoming parents.

I blasted worship music and praised God until the call came through that yes, we would travel to get our son. We arrived in Vietnam on my birthday, and what a memorable one it was.

When we returned home in November with our precious prize, after a nearly one-month stay in Vietnam, John began his new job in the company's New Jersey office, while his employers searched for a new office location in New York City.

What Hurts

When I am asked in front of my children how much I paid for them, it causes me pain. I feel that this intrusive question diminishes my children to the equivalent of puppies purchased at a pet store or possessions purchased with a credit card. And nobody's children should be considered possessions. Yet I have heard parents, adoptive and biological alike, say things like, "My daughter is my most prized possession." To me this indicates an unhealthy view of the relationship on the part of the possessor toward the one supposedly owned.

A pediatrician once asked me, "Are you the owner of these two adorable children?" This sounded odd to me. People own pets and cars and homes, not children.

Rather, adopted children are their parents' "own" in the sense that they are their personal and familial blessings from God to love, nurture and raise with His help, the same as the parents would any biological child. Besides, people do not belong to other people. The term suggests slavery. Our children, though we house, feed and dress them and make many of their decisions for them, are but on loan to us for a time. The only one any of us really belongs to is our heavenly Father, who created us and places us in our parents' care for a season.

My heart broke when my son overheard this inquiry from an acquaintance and even more so when he persisted in asking me how much he had cost. Words spoken around children—even children who appear engaged in another activity—are often heard and harbored in their minds.

Yet it seems that parents of biological children are never asked if their medical insurance covered the entire cost of their child's birth and delivery or if they had to dole out cash to pay for it.

Grace Given

Grace and forgiveness are essential in the face of hurtful things that others say to us. So too are they necessary for minor infractions that we endure, such as being cut off by another driver on the road. God expects a continuous stream of grace from us to others until we learn to give it freely and expediently.

However indelicately put, this question about the cost of adoption tells me that the asker wants to know if international adoption is really as expensive as he or she has heard or assumes that it is. Understanding this likely motivation does not excuse the poor judgment exercised by the person who cavalierly asks in front of my children how much I paid for them, but it does shed some light on why a person asks. And the truth is, people are correct to assume that foreign adoption can be costly.

People who want to know the costs associated with your adoption may have thought to pursue a foreign adoption themselves but assumed that they lacked the financial resources. Perhaps these individuals may not know anyone to ask about such things.

Handling It

God's primary concern for us, according to Romans 8:29, is that we follow a path that consistently shapes us into the image of Christ. That shaping requires that we heal from our old wounds and ways as well as endure trials that will stretch and shape us into our new godly selves. We therefore shouldn't be surprised by the repetition of challenges that God brings to us in those areas in which we are weak.

No one person's walk of faith is the same as another's. The impatient individual likely will find herself tested numerous times with situations that make her want to explode with frustration.

Someone whose identity is wrapped up in his image and his financial status may lose it all in order to learn humility and to find his true identity in Christ.

And then there is the person who is ultrasensitive, loathes confrontation and seems to be the frequent recipient of unkindness. Oh yes, that's me. Time after time I find myself at the mercy of words that target me as if they are loaded missiles. My inclination, when the pain becomes too great, is either to launch back at the person who insults me or to run for cover and nurse my wounds indefinitely. Neither approach is constructive. Rather than heed the words of Proverbs 15:1, which instruct us to use kind words to ward off wrath, I mouth off and invite more abuse. Rather than confront someone with Christlike love and truth, I become a coward. I withdraw to stew in the offense, and I feel like a victim.

The moment of confrontation that I experienced in the supermarket about the "cost" of my daughter blindsided me. The only thing I could think to do was to grab my wagon and walk away from this unwelcome intrusion into our lives. I wanted to protect my kids.

Since then, though, the question has come up without my children being present. In order to extend grace, I answer it with more questions, such as, "So are you thinking of adopting?" This is a good way to discover the motivation of a person's question. If I find that the person has thought about international or even domestic adoption, then, as an adoption advocate and as a Christian with a personal testimony of God's mighty provision, I share my story.

My husband and I always tell people who are genuinely interested in adoption that if they think the cost is too high, they don't know what God is capable of doing. He will not only make a way but will orchestrate every step of the process if He has a baby waiting somewhere in the world for them.

If people have impure motives, however, and their interest in the cost of our adoption is not genuine, then they won't care about our story. They're likely just nosy. But I always try to keep in mind the fact that these repetitive uncomfortable situations can become opportunities. Some of them may even be God's way of developing my character and maturing me in those areas in which I need the most work. I believe that God has His hand in the circumstances that challenge me and that He uses them for my good or for the good of another. But in order for Him to do so, I must do my part and ask Him to show me where He is at work: Is this question for my benefit, Lord? Are You at work trying to increase the faith of another? Do You mean for this other person to adopt too? If God uses me to plant a seed in another's heart that brings one child somewhere in the world into a loving home, then I consider the offense not only worth it but an honor.

Lucas has asked me a couple of times if we had to pay for him. I suspect the question was planted in his head by an intrusive stranger. It hurt my heart to think that he might consider himself a purchase, but we always have to give our children an answer to their questions.

Prayerfully, I told our son that God gave him to us as a gift. The perfect child for us lived across the globe, just waiting for parents. We went to a beautiful country and got to know its friendly people. And while we were enjoying all that, we got to receive the best gift of our lives: him. He seems satisfied with that answer.

Healing Questions

1. Have you ever been asked about the cost of your child's adoption? If so, how did it make you feel?

2. How have you seen God's hand at work in the details of your adoption plan?

3. Has your child ever asked you how much he or she "cost?" If so, what was your response? If not, how do you think you would respond should someone ever ask?

12

You're So Lucky!

Our two children have been called "lucky" across the globe, from Asia to the United States. In particular, when we were on our lengthy trip to Vietnam to adopt our son, everyone from the adoption agency staff to the orphanage caretakers to the hotel employees glowed with broad grins as they referred to Lucas as "lucky boy."

We knew that they meant that he was fortunate to be taken out of an orphanage and raised by parents who would provide him a better life, but how could they know whether Lucas was lucky to be with us? John and I didn't know. As new, anxious parents to a ten-month-old, we were quite concerned about what kind of job we would do as we brought up this child.

But more than this, each time Lucas received the "lucky boy" title, a sort of heart-wrenching, guilty feeling washed over me. In my mind's eye I saw all the other babies and children who had been left behind—one little girl in particular.

Before we traveled to Vietnam, as our scheduled departure date grew closer, we began to receive calls from our facilitator. A Vietnamese woman who had been born and raised in then Saigon and who now lived in the United States, she was to assist us in Ho Chi Minh City with our adoption process.

During one of our first conversations, she told us about another baby, a little girl she wanted us to consider adopting along with Lucas. She explained that the parents who had planned to adopt her had withdrawn their application at the last minute. The adoptive mother had become ill, and the couple felt that they couldn't take her. The facilitator told us that the baby had become "unlucky."

John and I were a bit caught off guard, to say the least. Yet at the same time, I felt excited at the thought of adopting a baby girl. My mind had always been set on a daughter, with my original plan having been to travel to China to make that happen. But then again, we both knew that we were overwhelmed enough at the prospect of parenting one child in just a few weeks. Was it possible that we could handle two six-month-old strangers at one time? Could I, the primary caretaker, focus on two babies the way I had envisioned that I would lavish all my attention on one?

Add to this the very real concern of provision for both children. Though God had provided for us mightily through Jenna and the new job my husband would start when we returned from Vietnam, we just did not have the required ten thousand dollars to make a second adoption happen. And, as new parents to be, we knew that we were unaware of what babies cost to care for.

Still, in my heart I wanted to know if this "double" adoption might be God's will for us, so I began to ask Him about it and then watched to see how He might lead.

As the weeks passed, our trip was cancelled and rescheduled repeatedly: The officials who were to perform our adoption ceremony were away at conferences. The Mekong Delta flooded, making the road leading to the orphanage impassable. The report was that at least one hundred children drowned in that flood. It broke our hearts to hear such news. With every cancellation came another call from our facilitator and the lure of the baby girl.

Still praying about what to do, I did not receive the peace I had hoped for. I felt torn, confused and responsible to "save" this baby. During one phone conversation I questioned our facilitator as to why another couple could not adopt her. She told me that Vietnam, unbeknownst to us, would be closing its doors to international adoptions and that it just wasn't possible to find this little girl parents in the short amount of time left before that happened. Talk about pressure!

John, on the other hand, was adamant that we should not take this second child. He did not feel led to do it, nor did he see a large sum of money coming our way to pay for a double adoption. Besides this, he told me that he felt overwhelmed at the idea of two babies at one time. With a heavy heart I realized that I could not allow this little girl to become a source of contention between us during what was already a stressful time. We had to be in agreement in order to proceed.

I had to surrender the temptation to force a situation that God had not sanctioned. Had He meant for us to have this child, He would have provided for us to take her in the same way that He had provided every step of the way for us to bring Lucas home. He could have rained down ten thousand dollars on our porch and given my husband and me the clear conviction to proceed had He desired to do so. This was not the case.

We finally made the trip to Vietnam, where we anxiously waited at the hotel in Ho Chi Minh City for the adoption details to be finalized. At long last the day came when with jangled nerves and racing hearts we traveled to the orphanage to meet our son for the first time. Sure, I had thought about the anonymous baby girl for weeks, but I had surrendered her to God's care. In my excitement to meet Lucas, the idea of her had faded somewhat.

Imagine my surprise when I found out that she was living in the same tiny baby house that my son lived in!

Our appointed translator sat on the floor a few feet away from where John and I had plunked ourselves down with Lucas and said to us, "This is unlucky baby." In an instant my joy turned into a jumble of shock, guilt, longing and suspicion.

I stared at the serene, delicate, tiny baby girl whom I was told was just a few weeks older than my son—now ten months old after all the delays that had prevented us from traveling earlier to Vietnam. My heart ached to think of what might become of her. Though I knew I shouldn't have, I asked to hold her. The translator obliged and handed her to me.

I smelled her baby smell, stroked her soft skin and brushed back her wispy, black hair. And I prayed for parents for her too. And not only did I see her this one time, but I saw her time and again as the official ceremony to formally adopt Lucas was repeatedly delayed and we made more fourteen-hour round-trip visits from Ho Chi Minh City to the orphanage. With each visit I could not stop myself from holding her, touching her, trying to interact with her. I ached for her and began to believe in the possibility that we could, in fact, bring her home too.

Then one afternoon our facilitator called us to a meeting in the lobby of the hotel where we were staying and flat out told us that we had to take this baby girl. I felt stunned, and my stomach twisted in knots as our facilitator explained that babies were virtually unadoptable beyond the age of two. If Vietnam were about to shut down adoptions, "unlucky" couldn't make it out. By the time the country reopened, she wouldn't make it out.

My heart felt as if it were tearing to pieces as I absorbed this information. Just two years old? This meant then that the very first children we had watched playing together at the sandy entrance to the orphanage had no chance of being adopted. They had been a tousle-haired boy of about six years old and a beautiful, dark-skinned, smiling little girl a bit younger than that.

"What happens to them?" I wanted to know.

"They turn them out of the orphanages at fourteen," said our facilitator. "The girls become prostitutes, and the boys collect garbage to live on," she added with a completely flat expression. Horrified, I imagined filthy, teenage boys in the crowded and dirty streets in search of abandoned, partially eaten meals. And it nearly brought me to tears to think that "unlucky," along with numerous other sweet girls, might barely reach the onset of puberty before their youth and vibrancy would be drained from them as they sold their bodies on the busy, narrow alleyways of Ho Chi Minh City.

I went numb as the facilitator then offered us a "discount" to get us to say yes. Anger began to well up inside me as she cavalierly offered to knock off a thousand dollars of the ten thousand on the price of a human life in order to "sweeten the deal," she said.

I wanted then and there to dial up an affluent family member and plead for the money just to get this baby out of this environment in which people would negotiate a sale price for her. As I gave my husband the most pathetic, begging look I could muster, the facilitator announced, "You will come back in three months to pick her up."

I knew now, however, that we were looking at an additional fifteen thousand dollars to adopt this second baby as well as another trip that my husband likely would not be able to make once he started his new job. I began to realize that this forced adoption situation was not from the hand of God, and I knew that I did not trust our facilitator. I wanted only to do that which God had led us to do, which was to take our son home.

When we visited that orphanage for the last time, we were given a picture. The small photo showed three smiling caretakers standing together, each holding up a baby—one was Lucas, one the couple's we had traveled with and the third "unlucky."

What Hurts

To pressure and manipulate a couple into adopting a baby is hurtful. To lead them to believe that they are the only hope in the world to change a child's "bad luck" when they obviously cannot take on the fiduciary or emotional responsibility of his or her care is wrong. And pressuring prospective parents over and over again to do this is a painful and difficult hardship to put a couple through. It robs two people of some of the joy that they have for the way in which God has orchestrated their one adoption and for the baby He has already blessed them with.

I've since learned that an adoption agency representative who tells people that children over the age of two are unadoptable is not telling the truth. While there is a preference for babies among adoptive couples, large numbers of adoptive parents are happy with and even prefer to adopt older children.

We were told that Vietnam would shut down adoptions completely, but in fact, it would close its doors only to the United States, not to all nations, so that was simply a lie.

Furthermore, *ordering* a couple to adopt a baby and trying to strike a deal for that baby is unconscionable.

It hurt a lot, particularly as a Christian, to hear the baby girl continually referred to as "unlucky." While the word "luck" is described in the dictionary as "chance, accident, and fortune"— some random good thing coming from some unknown, intangible force—it can be anathema to the Christian. Many of us believe to the core of our beings that "every good gift and every perfect gift is from above" (James 1:17). And everything that is not good or perfect about our lives isn't "unlucky" but rather allowed by God.

God chose our son for us and us for him. In addition, He knew that we weren't meant to have the little girl whom our facilitator called "unlucky baby." He is mightier than one cancelled adoption. God created that little girl, and He holds her in the palm of His hand.

As my children grow and hear people call them lucky for having been adopted, it confuses them. For one thing, it perpetuates the untruth that fate and chance bring them good things or bad. And it also can make them feel as if they should have this incredible appreciation for my husband and me for adopting them when we don't want them to experience any sense of indebtedness to us. And believe me, in their young minds and with their concepts of "luck," parents don't make them lucky, for we have the power to restrict, prohibit or frustrate their good times. Rather, lucky to our kids resembles winning a shiny orange goldfish in a plastic bag at a carnival or finding money or a toy under their pillows after they lose a tooth.

Grace Given

We need to give grace and respect to people of other cultures. When we set out on an adoption journey to a foreign country, we are exposed to all sorts of strange sights, unusual sounds and frames of reference unlike ours. The concept of luck can be a significant and powerful force to peoples of other lands.

Anything from animal symbols to colors to certain gemstones can exude good luck, as they sometimes can for people here in the United States. But good fortune is also considered by some to be delivered through a multitude of gods or dead relatives. Even death can be considered lucky.

One afternoon, as we waited in the agony of those weeks for our son's release from the orphanage, we were escorted by our facilitator to an elaborate temple. In front of the ornate building, we saw a procession of people wearing white, surrounded by what appeared to be a tall chariot that inched by.

"This is the funeral of a small boy," our facilitator told us. "We are very lucky to be here for this."

In a foreign country we can encounter so many things that fly in the face of reality as we have always known it. Our beliefs, values, expectations, sense of injustice or the macabre can be dismissed by the people who have our child and who have the power to either release the child to us or to change their minds. We may find ourselves putting up with a lot for fear of offending the ones who hold that power over our adoption.

Even in the United States, what people call luck sometimes flies in the face of our Christian values. Lotteries and sweepstakes and promotions that are used to get people to "try their luck" are cases in point. People may scoff at those who are "unlucky in love" or at skilled sports professionals relying on "lucky" charms. "Luck" is a highly ingrained cultural word and used often in every culture.

As such, grace must be given to our aunt or neighbor or even to that stranger who tells our child that he or she is lucky to have been adopted. I believe that well-meaning people say this to adopted children because they consider your child's alternative to adoption a bleak one.

In Vietnam we were told that the future prospects for children who were not adopted were dismal, and that for one reason: without parents children did not have a legal name. Without a legal name they couldn't be counted among those who had a right to employment. And without employment how could a person eke out a living?

If this be true, grace must be given to adoption personnel who work hard to secure orphaned children with freedom, education and health care.

Handling It

We must never insult or correct another nation's perceptions. Though we may feel a strong urge at times to express ourselves regarding certain ways that our adoption is being handled, we need to be careful. Self-restraint, faith and trust in God are essential. After all, we can't control the system or the people around us who have the baby that our heart has longed for.

It's best to stick to common ground—love for the child you've come to receive and thanks for the hospitality you are shown in a foreign country.

It is not a good idea to tell people of another culture that we don't believe in luck and to stop calling our son a lucky boy. When we return home, we can point out to friends and relatives who call our child lucky that it is we as parents who have been blessed by God with the child He has brought into our lives.

As for the little baby girl whom I remember with such clarity in my mind's eye, when I think of her I try not to think, *What if?* but rather, *Why not?* What I mean is that there is no reason on earth that God might not change her circumstances and keep her from the fate that our facilitator had insisted awaited her. I had to let go of the responsibility for this little girl's future. God had called me to adopt Lucas, and the other children's futures were in His capable hands.

Perhaps the couple who cancelled the little girl's adoption weren't the right parents for her. Or perhaps the mother was healed of her illness and returned for the child. Maybe a couple from France or Canada adopted her, or perhaps even a couple from the United States who wanted an older child. It could have been that God wanted us to pray for her though not raise her. Then again, God could have plans for her to grow up in her native country, where things will improve for orphaned children, or He may use her to become a light and a source of strength and hope for other abandoned children. Unlucky? I don't think so.

Healing Questions

1. If you've adopted internationally, have you experienced cultural differences that made you uncomfortable? If so, how have you handled them?

2. How has your faith in God been put in action during difficult circumstances in your adoption process?

3. Has anyone ever called your child "lucky" for having been adopted? What has been or what would be your reaction to this?

PART 3

Transracial Family and Ethnic Offenses

13

Why's He Sweating? You'd Think He'd Be Used to the Heat!

On one of those dog days of summer, I left church after our service. Around one o'clock in the afternoon, it must have been over ninety degrees outside. I rushed an eighteen-month-old Lucas through the scorching heat to our car in the parking lot.

The reflection of that ball of fire in the sky on all the glass, aluminum and chrome surrounding me seared my eyes, forcing them half closed. The steam rising from my car gave it a ghostly shimmer that made it seem a dancing apparition instead of a solid, two-thousand pound machine.

A sweaty, uncomfortable Lucas wailed as I hurried past a fellow churchgoer, the husband of a friend. His car sat parked next to mine.

"Gosh, Lucas is really hot," I said to Phil, who watched us. I hoped that placing my baby in the car before it was cooled off and moving wouldn't render him unconscious. That's when Phil cavalierly remarked, "Why's he sweating? You'd think he'd be used to the heat!"

Without a doubt, Ho Chi Minh City, Vietnam, from mid-October through early November feels to one not indigenous to such parts sort of like a sauna. Though this season is referred to as the dry one in which constant, heavy rains abate, the term is relative, depending on where in the world you live.

Within five minutes of venturing outdoors into the steamy, dirty, crowded streets, it feels as if the shower you took in the hotel bathroom never happened.

Even though I have lived through decades of grueling, humid New York summers, after which I have never altogether dried out until well into autumn, I never felt anything quite as intense as the Vietnamese tropical heat. In addition to that, my perimenopause along with my body's extra bit of cushioning (as compared to the average slim Vietnamese woman) made my endless damp discomfort all the greater.

In all my "new mom" pictures, my curly, frizzy hair resembled steel wool set above a shiny forehead. I also sported a rash on my face from constantly swiping at the trickling beads of perspiration that tickled my upper lip. Other than lipstick, the makeup I had brought with me on my journey remained unused.

I found no reprieve anywhere indoors either, except at our hotel. One did not hear the rattle and hum of air conditioners from residences or businesses. In fact, most shops, other than those at the mall, were tiny, open-air storefronts.

As we walked through the city, I marveled at the hot soup poured into bowls by roadside merchants who prepared for lunch. I longed for a good old American movie theater, supermarket or restaurant that would welcome me with the chill of a meat locker.

I noticed early into our stay in Vietnam that the people didn't seem to sweat. Young women covered in spotless white pants and matching long-sleeved tunics reflected modesty and purity as they scooted by on motorbikes amidst the throng of humanity. They appeared so put together and dry. In the meantime, I poured embarrassing buckets of moisture from sweat glands I hadn't even known existed.

But I suppose our body temperature adjusts to the weather to which it is exposed over time. My family who now lives in Florida visits us in New York and complains that they are freezing when the temperature dips below sixty degrees.

I've also known people from drier parts of the United States who have relocated to New York and then moved back to where they are originally from, grateful, in the words of one former coworker of mine, to have left behind "those horrid New York summers."

What Hurts

If there is anything that husbands and fathers (both of which my friend Phil is) should know about mothers who struggle with crying infants, it is that they should either man up or move on. I know this sounds harsh, but it is true. During our stressful moments it is never helpful for us, nor do we appreciate it, when a person hangs back and minimizes our struggles.

Frankly, Phil's comment, though I believe not intended to offend, struck me at the time as both hurtful and misinformed.

Lucas had been home with us for at least seven months before Phil commented on how the heat shouldn't bother him. Since Lucas had arrived in New York in late fall, his first exposure to his new climate was that of chilly to progressively colder weather. His body adapted to plummeting temperatures, wind and snow before he experienced his first summer in New York. By June, he was no longer accustomed to life in the sauna-like conditions of a tropical environment.

Phil's comment seemed to imply that because Lucas is of Vietnamese heritage, he should be able to comfortably endure intense heat—no matter where he lives. If that were true, wouldn't it also be true that winter would not be his favorite season of the year, as it has been since he was a baby?

Truth be told, Lucas has always reacted to the heat with lots of sweating. During our first summer with him, he had extreme meltdowns during outings we went on. It took my husband and me a while to figure out that once these started, we had to immediately return home and strip him down to his diaper. His disposition would go from night to day as he cooled off, settled down and resumed his usual, happy, playful self.

What Phil's comment said to me was that my child is different from others because of his race. It implied that he stood apart from all the other hot, sweaty kids in the ninety-plus heat in a blacktop parking lot. It is this inference of him as separate from others, this misinformed judgment of what he is like and how he should behave, that is at the heart of the matter. That is what gets my back up and my defenses readied.

My tongue wanted to lash out, "Listen, he doesn't live in Vietnam anymore, and can't you as a father appreciate the fact that he is miserable?" For that was another thing. Phil's cavalier comment to me as a frazzled mother with a crying baby hurt my feelings. I thought it would have been the Christian thing to do for him to open my car door or to start my car and get the air conditioning going while I strapped Lucas into his seat or to even offer me a word of compassion. After all, I felt, we had just prayed and worshiped and shared fellowship together, and we had come out of the church ready, so I thought, to put our faith into renewed practice.

Grace Given

How much more do we expect in speech and action from those who profess Christianity than we do from those who are not Christians?

Often, I have discovered, quite a lot. Throughout my walk with the Lord, I have had to learn painful lessons about how to curb my expectations of others, in particular of Christians.

Though the Bible is filled with mandates to the believer on how we are to behave toward other believers, I understand that all of us are capable of all kinds of sinful attitudes and behaviors. Yet my feelings of disappointment with those who are aware of these mandates always seem to be greater than with nonbelievers.

It is wrong to hold other Christians to a standard of excellence and perfection, because doing so means that we expect others to be

Christ, not Christlike. Our whole Christian lives are about allowing God to transform us into the image of Christ. I have to remember that we are all at various stages in this process.

For the most part, I have known great love, kindness and acceptance from fellow Christians. Giving grace to Phil for his comment was important for me, because this same person who made that comment is one of the only persons to have met us at the airport when we landed in New York with Lucas.

It was well after midnight when we stepped off the last of our plane rides in a string of flights from Asia to New York after our three-and-a-half-week stay in Vietnam to adopt Lucas. I staggered into the cool, autumn air in the same clothing I had put on two days earlier, now rumpled and covered in an odorous assortment of baby food, formula and sweat.

I had dreamed of this moment as one in which we would bask in the love and support of family and friends who would hold welcome-home signs and balloons. They would all rush up to Lucas with oohs and aahs and would kiss and hug him with tears in their eyes. But as it was nearing midnight on a weeknight, and as our family all lived a good hour or more away, this did not happen. Instead, Phil, joined by another Christian friend of ours, were the only two to greet us at the airport when we arrived with our new son.

I can't forget Phil's faithfulness and kindness in being there for us that night. Whenever I think of the time we brought Lucas home, I see Phil standing there, a shadowy-looking yet very real brother in Christ who said, "Looks like you've got your hands full."

Handling It

I'm sure that I have a few scars on my tongue from having bitten it on numerous occasions. On that particular blistering day, the fact that I had just come out of church where I had worshiped and prayed to God helped restrain me from becoming an unloving hypocrite.

The distraction too of getting my son out of the blazing sun and into his car seat helped prevent me from spewing unkind words.

Then the moment was gone and with it the impulse to react with unkind words.

But I could have responded. It would have been neither unkind nor unloving to say that my son was no longer used to the heat in the way in which he once was. That would have been calm and factual.

One of the main things to remember when it comes to others' hurtful words is that our hurt feelings usually boil down to what we actually hear people say. Often as we learn to be a good parent, and in particular one who loves and protects a child of another race, it isn't just a comment or two that puts us off. Rather it is the seemingly endless stream of minor infractions by those whom we feel should care about our feelings as well as by strangers who inject themselves into our daily routine that make us feel as if we are drowning in a sea of hurt. Then, all of a sudden, one more comment becomes the proverbial straw that breaks the camel's back. What we hear at our breaking point is more than the comment: it is a compilation of the many slights and jabs of pain for our children that becomes unbearable. It is at this point that our natural, fleshly response is to fight.

But God is so good to use the children He brings into our lives to illuminate those areas of our hearts that need work. He has shown me that I should try to understand others' frames of reference better and should not expect everyone to fully understand mine. And I should not anticipate that every other Christian will ask for God's approval before they utter a word.

Healing Questions

1. Have you found yourself expecting better behavior from Christians than from others who cross your path? If so, why do you think this is?

2. How can you curb your expectations in light of the fact that we are all being transformed into the image of Christ in our own time?

3. How have your children been used in your life to show you areas of your own heart that need work?

14

She's Such a Little China Doll!

We returned to the United States from China with our precious bundle, whom we had named Olivia Autumn, on the eve of Thanksgiving. Olivia, because I liked the name and because our baby girl looked like an Olivia in her referral photo. I hadn't known at the time that the name is derived from "olive" or "olive tree" and means "fertile." And Autumn, because her Chinese name had been translated to us as "cool autumn."

How befitting our homecoming date seemed, since we had so much to be thankful for with this new life whom God had given us to love and cherish.

The next day's scheduled Thanksgiving celebration was to take place at the house of one of my five sisters, about a thirty-five-minute drive from us.

Of course we were all quite jet lagged from the long flight home and from the thirteen-hour time difference between China and New York. And unlike Lucas when we had brought him home, poor Olivia had not slept well on the plane at all.

Tired and overwhelmed by all the brand-new sights, smells and sounds around her and slow to bond with us, she was quiet and withdrawn. But I did not want to miss the holiday with my family and the opportunity to show Olivia off to her new aunts, uncles, cousins and grandpa.

I dressed my beautiful baby in a frilly dress, tights, shiny black patent-leather shoes and a hair bow. I may have been exhausted, but with joy in my heart, I walked into my sister's house, where Olivia was greeted with cautious fanfare, given her flat expression.

When we all gathered around the dining table for dinner, I propped Olivia on my lap, where she sat motionless and silent. My sister Patty's triplet boys, born just a day before the estimated birthdate we were given for Olivia, were, unlike her, not only able to walk but to run at thirteen months. As they tore up the house, Patty sat across the table from me and stared at Olivia in what I imagined to be disbelief.

"She's like a little china doll," she said with a faint smile.

Though I knew Olivia might have been too fatigued and even frightened to move, I beamed with pride at my sister. It felt so good that my long-time dream to have a daughter was finally a reality. And my special, adorable little china doll was all dressed up and leaning on my lap like a tiny plaything.

And so the references to Olivia as a little china doll continued through the holidays, at church, at birthday parties and at play dates. I enjoyed each and every one of them as I continued to dress her up and show her off.

About a year after we returned home with her, our family attended a fall festival in our town that had an abundance of fun rides for the kids.

I carried Olivia, and together John, Lucas and I all trudged up a seemingly never-ending staircase that led to the top of a huge slide. My husband sat down with Lucas on his lap. When I tried to arrange the thick, course blanket I had been given to sit down on, I turned to the teenage boy who oversaw the slide and asked him to hold Olivia for a moment. With great care he took hold of her and cradled her in his arms as though she were a newborn. She stared up at him.

"She's like a baby china doll!" he remarked.

I laughed because she did look like a little doll in his arms, and he gazed down on her as though he could not believe how petite and serene she appeared. And nobody else had a baby like her.

What Hurts

Me. I should never have gloated over how others saw my child as a china doll.

That still, expressionless demeanor that made her so doll-like had cut me to the core with worry in China. Though Olivia would transform and blossom into a fun-loving, happy child over time, her likeness to a doll as a baby should have given me pause for concern. Out of the house our daughter's somber demeanor was likely borne out of some fear, overstimulation and an innate reserved personality in new situations. But behind closed doors she seemed anything but a doll. In fact, she appeared to be unhappy much of the time, and she woke up every night in the wee hours in tears, having no "off" switch. She was not the ultrahappy, self-entertaining child Lucas had been at that age, and I struggled to manage my time between the two children as I got to know this little girl and accept that she was not a female version of Lucas.

Yet everywhere we went Olivia wore yet another beautiful outfit and gazed silently at people, and she still received her china doll "compliments," which I continued to enjoy. In light of what I knew, however, it was wrong of me to feel good about how others viewed her as somewhat of a pretty little toy.

Although the word "china" refers to the porcelain out of which these delicate dolls are made, it seemed to me that people often used the term "china doll" as a racial reference to Olivia as well. I have never heard people differentiate race when they call a child a doll except in the case of the little Chinese girl. But "china doll" is, in my experience, so freely tossed around when it refers to a female Chinese baby or child.

Throughout the years, Olivia has received a number of Chinese dolls as gifts meant to celebrate her ethnicity and birth country. Many of them are quite delicate and too dainty to drag around the house by one arm as little girls are wont to do with their dolls. Also, they do not feel soft and cuddly enough for trips in the car or for bedtime, because they are mostly made of porcelain and better suited to placement on a shelf or in a cabinet. Behind glass they sit in our house while they exhibit the faintest of expressions on their powder-white faces that surround tiny, red lips. They wear colorful silk kimonos tied by sashes, and their shiny, black hair is neatly held up by slender, smooth, wooden sticks.

When Olivia is given one of these gifts, I wonder what she sees. Even though she is proud to be Chinese, the dolls have not interested her in the least.

Olivia's favorite dolls have been the ones that, frankly, have made me want to cringe when she took them out with us. Their hair always resembled a tangled mess that covered faces scrawled with crayon. She liked to carry them around in the buff, and oftentimes one of their eyes would stay shut. She would not wrap her babies in any of the soft, pretty baby-doll blankets she had been given but rather would make use of my most tattered, stained dish towels to cover them up.

Olivia is a bit unconventional. As she has grown, she has developed into a sporty tomboy who refuses to submit to the stereotype once placed on her of china doll. And at all of three years old, she put her tiny foot down about being primped in ruffles, lace and bows. Give her a pair of comfy jeans and a T-shirt instead.

I wonder if some of it has to do with having heard people call her "that little china doll" for years. It must confuse a child to be referred to as such. After all, how can the young Chinese girl identify with a powdered, porcelain, pouting, red-lipped image that's supposed to represent her "people" as it stares back at her through glass?

Grace Given

Sometimes we all lack awareness regarding the things we say and how those things may affect others.

When I gazed upon my daughter, I saw this tiny, fourteen-pound baby at thirteen months old who stayed still and quiet much of the time. Olivia's mere presence made it easy for me to slip on lenses through which I perceived her as a doll. The commonness of the phrase "china doll" and the way in which others used it to describe her made it all the easier to attribute the term to her. I perpetuated the stereotype because it was widespread and seemed to fit.

All of us are capable of stereotyping; it isn't just when we have negative views of other cultures that we engage in this behavior. Sometimes we mean well—we even mean our perspective to be a compliment—but that so-called flattering remark is borne out of ignorance or convenience and does harm, not good.

We all learn how to be inaccurate and to label people from all sorts of sources. Sometimes our attempts to make sense of such a big, diverse, complicated and ever-changing world results in our drawing language and ideas from myths and well-worn phrases that we've grown up with or become accustomed to. When we do this, we fit things and people into neat little packages of understanding.

Take, for instance, the belief in astrology, or what the dictionary describes as "a pseudoscience claiming that the moon, sun, and stars affect human affairs and can be used to foretell the future."[1] This pseudoscience causes some to try and make sense of others based on their astrological signs or to decipher what kinds of supposed traits they have based on when they were born and how the moon, stars and sun all lined up in the heavens at the person's birth. It's a way of taking all humanity and compartmentalizing it into twelve neat and predictable groups.

There are other, less innocuous ways in which we engage in pursuing myths about ourselves. The Internet and magazines are filled with examples of how we are "teased" into doing so. Have you ever seen articles given titles like "What Your Hairstyle Really Reveals About Your Personality" or "What Your Favorite Colors Say About the Career You Should Choose"? From time to time I have perused these kinds of articles out of curiosity. I usually end up scoffing at them, but admittedly I "bite" when it comes to the possibility of finding out more about who I am or how I am viewed by others. These things cause us to mythologize personality traits and abilities about ourselves and others based upon assumptions some writers make in order to publish material.

And we can hold onto myths about ourselves that are imposed upon us by those whom we encounter. Some may be positive, while others have negative connotations. For instance, I recently ran across an article at a website, *Black Enterprise*. In an article entitled "You Don't Say! 10 Unbelievable Myths About Black People," author Amber McKynzie attempts to dispel the myths that aggravate African-Americans such as, "All black people can sing," or they can "run fast," or they "all look alike."[2] Even if meant as a positive reference to an ethnic group of people, these urban legends obviously still annoy, are erroneous and skew people's view of others, perhaps themselves and other cultures.

Even myths about God get thrown into everyday verbiage. Many of us have heard the phrase "See, God punished you!" after we have said something unsavory about another person or let out a four-letter word and then suddenly tripped in the street. The person then instantaneously refers to a punishing God who will make us pay for our transgressions. Just last week I shared with a few people that my back windshield inexplicably burst into a million pieces while I was driving to work. One person commented, "Maybe that was God punishing you." Though we are taught that God allows unpleasant and even painful events to occur in our lives, we also know that accidents and other things that we don't understand happen to us and even to our vehicles. But don't we have to fight against the concept that perhaps these myths that people toss at us are true? Even for a split second? Admittedly, I was happy to hear another person add, "Perhaps God protected you, because it happened at a stoplight rather than when you were driving, and you weren't harmed."

Myth is so ingrained in our culture that things like numbers and names can be associated with imposing bad things upon us. Many buildings do not have a thirteenth floor. The other day a Facebook friend of mine begged someone to like her page because she currently had 666 likes and couldn't stand the thought of having the number of the devil associated with her author page.

These myths and stereotypes are just that: myths and stereotypes. They have no basis in truth, but they give us simple categories through which we try to understand our complex world.

Handling It

Over time I realized that though the china-doll reference was meant by others with no ill will and even as a compliment, I had to dispute it. I did so with a lot of humor, because humor is a good way to defuse tension when we want to correct someone in a nonthreatening manner.

It is our responsibility as parents to adopted children to protect them from being labeled. They cannot do this for themselves, and people, including we parents, should not feel at liberty to pin any labels on them. As it is written in First Corinthians 13:7 (NIV), love "always protects."

The china-doll comment has occurred with much less frequency as my daughter has grown into an adventurous, athletic tomboy. But when I do hear it, I may laugh and say, "She certainly is beautiful, but she does a lot more than a doll!"

I find too that my children are old enough now for me to incorporate them into these exchanges. I can now agree with the person who says this that they mean Olivia has beauty but then turn to my daughter and ask her, "Do you think that you're a china doll?" She will always shake her head and respond with a firm no. This is one way I can express to the person that I understand what they mean but that there might be a better way to say it than to compare my child to a doll.

Once when Lucas was about four years old, someone almost endearingly called him "a little china man." I asked my son, who was peacefully sitting on a swing at the time, "Are you a little china man?" Instantly he replied, "No, I'm a little boy, and I'm from Vietnam. My sister is from China."

And when my children are exposed to others who refer to them or to other Asian-Americans as oriental, we understand that the person using the term is not purposefully being offensive. They do not seem to know that the term dates back to "orientalism," when Asians were considered "savages" and when Asian women were all seen as sexual objects. I do not even have to coach my kids to politely correct the person as they automatically say, "We are Asian," or, "I think you mean to say Asian instead."

It's the same for those moments in which others will exclaim something like, "My, they are tall!" In some cases, though not in all, as with people who haven't seen my children for a time, it's as though the person is impressed with my children's height, because they seem to be thinking, "Aren't Asians usually short?" Lucas and Olivia usually stare at those who say this with a frown, and one of them might say, "Of course, *anybody* can be tall." It's Olivia though, who likes to share, "The tallest person in the world is Asian!" She is referring to a documentary we once watched together. The girl she speaks about may be *one* of the tallest worldwide and sadly has a disorder that causes her tremendous height, but people don't seem to be aware of this. I love Olivia for telling them this, because it usually silences the other person, ending the conversation.

Healing Questions

1. Have you or has anyone you know ever labeled your child with regard to his or her ethnicity? What did the person say?

2. If your child has been labeled, how did you feel about it at the time, and how do you feel about it now?

3. How does using humor work for you in correcting others or in trying to change their perspectives?

15

Hello, Little Glasshoppa!

The front door burst open. Lucas' cousin had arrived for a visit. A mischievous kid for as long I can remember, he strode inside with his usual cocky grin, my sister not far behind him. "Hey, Patrick," I greeted him.

"Hi," he said as he leaned in to give me a kiss on the cheek. "Where's Lucas?"

"In the family room playing Legos," I replied.

Lucas, a serious Lego builder, didn't even look up as Patrick rounded the corner and walked into the family room.

Patrick snuck up behind my son, ruffled his hair in a playful manner and said, "Hello, little glasshoppa!" Well, this got my back up; I was ready to object to the reference and perhaps even to scold Patrick for using it. But then I wondered if I were being too sensitive. It was another one of those moments in which I had to decide if my child was actually the recipient of a racial slight and whether or not I should take issue with it.

We all know that a grasshopper is an insect. But besides this, the word is used as a reference to one who is under the tutelage of another who is older, wiser and more proficient in skill or endeavor.

This second definition of grasshopper found its way into twenty-first-century expression through a popular 1970s television series called *Kung Fu*.

Kung Fu followed the adventures of a Shaolin monk named Kwai Chang Caine, who traveled through the American Old West in search of his half brother. Flashbacks are used to recall lessons that Caine had received from his childhood training in a Shaolin monastery, where he was accepted after the death of his last parental figure, his Chinese maternal grandfather.

In one of these flashbacks, Caine's blind teacher Master Po tells his student, "Close your eyes. What do you hear?"

"I hear the water; I hear the birds," replies the young Caine.

"Do you hear your own heartbeat?" asks Po.

"No," replies Caine.

"Do you hear the grasshopper that is at your feet?" asks Po.

"Old man, how is it that you hear these things?" the young Caine wants to know.

"Young man, how is it that you do not?" the old man replies.

Thus was born the reference to Caine as the young "grasshopper," used throughout the remainder of the show, as well as the term's use in our culture's verbiage.

But the term seems to have been used as one, perhaps, of endearment by the old, blind mentor for his young pupil. When it comes to the *Kung Fu* series as a commentary on racial issues affecting Asians, it can be said that it had a rather positive effect. For one thing, it drew attention to the fact that there has been racial discrimination toward Asians for centuries. As Caine grew from a young pupil into adulthood, the series writers portrayed him as the recipient of racial slurs, prejudice and even hatred. But Caine always came out on top, using the skills and instruction taught him by his former master to right a wrong, to defend his and his people's honor and to clearly convey that he was neither weak nor willing to endure the gross injustices that others intended to inflict upon him. And many viewers of all ethnicities felt outraged by his pain, while they also cheered his victories over his tormentors.

This show, broadcast during the 1970s, reveals a consciousness of a nation at that time that was both exploring and exposing racial offenses and discrimination. Examining one race's pain and frustration with *Kung Fu* and creating a likeable, honorable character whom all kinds of people related to and wanted to see as a champion was, in my estimation, a good thing.

What Hurts

I did not respond *specifically* to Patrick's use of "glasshoppa" in reference to my son. I wanted to think about it before I formed an opinion about the matter. When I did finally ponder the comment, I realized that what hurt wasn't the fact that my son was called a grasshopper. A lot of people in my age group have watched the *Kung Fu* series, remember it and have the phrase "grasshopper" etched into their minds. It's like that with a lot of things we are exposed to.

I have also heard the phrase tossed around when someone tries to teach another something that he or she is good at. I don't believe it is meant as a racial slur or a terribly derogatory reference.

But what I found objectionable was the pseudo-Asian *pronunciation* of the word. What Lucas can grasp (although maybe not in that exact moment) is the phony Asian accent. My concern is that it could confuse and insult him. Neither my husband and I nor my children confront red-haired, freckled kids while impersonating an Irish brogue to say, "Top o' the mornin' to ya!" Nor do we approach African-Americans and say, "Yo, bro!" In fact, I don't hear others say things in supposedly ethnic dialects to non-Asian groups. Maybe they do. But it seems that even though we live in a diverse community and there are millions of Asian-Americans living in this country, it is Asians that bear the brunt of a lot of this kind of insulting play on words that depicts them as incapable of pronouncing words correctly.

Actually, it ties into a prevalent way of deriding those of Asian descent: that of mocking the Chinese language with the phrase "ching chong." This making up of Chinese words is as a "pejorative sometimes employed by speakers of English to mock or play on the Chinese language, people of Chinese ancestry, or other East Asians who may be mistaken for Chinese that reside in Western countries."[1]

Asian-Americans have been dealing with ongoing incidences of "ching chong" throughout history. It prevails today with highly visible situations such as when Rosie O'Donnell of *The View* and conservative political commentator Rush Limbaugh used it on air in recent years. Their mockery of the Chinese caused a stir among Asian-Americans. Representative Judy Chu of California said that Limbaugh's words were the same as those the Chinese have heard for 150 years as they endured racial discrimination while at the same time they "were called racial slurs, were spat upon in the streets, derided in the halls of Congress and even brutally murdered."

As far as O'Donnell is concerned, she apologized to "those people who felt hurt." But Jeff Yang, who tracks Asian and Asian-American trends for a market research firm said that O'Donnell's apology really should have been for "spreading and encouraging ignorance." O'Donnell's insensitive response was to warn the public that "there's a good chance I'll do something like that again, probably next week, not on purpose. Only 'cause it's how my brain works."[2]

This kind of situation—in which we feel hurt for and ready to defend our children—is similar to others in which part of what we hear may not be a direct slur or form of discrimination (and we always must consider the source of a comment), but another aspect of it is.

For instance, when someone I know took his first look at my Vietnamese son, home with us for only a short time, he asked if Lucas had ever eaten a dog. My initial feeling was that of extreme hurt for what I interpreted as a rejection of this beautiful baby that I was now thrilled to be a mother to. Right along with it was outrage at what to me smacked of what I referred to earlier as orientalism. Only savages would eat a dog, right?

We live in a society in which many people have free reign to post their offensive ignorance in public forums. I have happened across YouTube videos in which people go on for over two minutes with some of the most offensive, disgusting and profane Asian racial slurs you can imagine. I'd never even heard many of them. In one the creator said he would continue to do videos for all the various ethnicities. He said that people shouldn't get offended, because his comments were "just words." Just words. If you've read this far into this book, I know that you have taken away from it the enormous impact of those collections of letters strung together. The tongue, after all (and the printed page, I might add), has the power of life and death (see Prov. 18:21).

Grace Given

As I have said, transracial families must always consider the source when they believe that they've heard an offensive comment about their child's culture or ethnicity. I must say that in most cases it is easier to offer grace to an eight-year-old like Patrick than to an adult. I don't know where Patrick picked up his usage of the grasshopper phrase, and in particular its pseudo-Asian pronunciation, but it was probably from an adult or even perhaps from a source like the Internet.

As far as Patrick is concerned, I don't think his intention was to be mean to Lucas or to cause him harm. He loves to be with Lucas, and from what I have observed of their relationship, he wouldn't hurt him on purpose. Perhaps he himself has been called a grasshopper or even a "glasshoppa" by others.

I have also heard the phrase tossed around, albeit without the phony Asian accent, when someone tries to teach another something that he or she is good at. I honestly don't believe that in most cases the term is used in a negative way.

And yes, I had to extend grace to the person who asked if my baby had ever eaten a dog. While it may not have been the most appropriate thing to inquire of new parents to a much-loved, nearly toothless infant from another country, I had to consider the source in this case as well. You see, earlier in the book I described how when we were approached by our adoption agency with the possibility of travel to Vietnam for a child, my initial thoughts were of a country I knew little about except a controversial, horrible war. I can say that some of the images of war and suffering were conjured up in my mind in the moment and that I had an immediate sensation of distaste at the thought of going to such a place for a child. But after our adoption journey there, I came away with a lasting portrait of a beautiful and fascinating country filled with warm people and beautiful children along with the desire to one day return there with my family to show my son his birth country. Perhaps this man's impressions of Vietnam are simply shaped by what he has heard.

As for individuals who share offensive and disturbing content online, I am angered by them. But I also do not know what hurt and misguidance they have experienced in their lives. Ultimately, I feel sorry for them, and I pray that people around them will speak words of truth and wisdom into their lives.

Handling It

I've gone through some basic principles as to how to forgive and handle hurtful words. But I know that the comments involving a child's race are among the most difficult to deal with. These aren't little uh-oh moments that we experience because we may have said or done something insensitive ourselves. They are not intrusive questions about how much we paid for our adoptions or whether we have children whom we gave birth to at home. Nor are they directed at us, the parents. Rather, they specifically target our child of a race different from ours. These words can reek of a lack of acceptance for or a mockery of our child and an entire race. And as parents, we begin to develop an understanding of what it might feel like for our kids to carry around the burden of labels taped to their foreheads as they navigate the course of their young, impressionable everyday lives. We hurt deeply for our kids as well as for others who experience the same types of disrespect.

But as in all situations involving hurtful words, we must first keep our emotions at bay. We do not turn hostile and unleash our wrath on the person who makes the comment. This is ungodly. And next, we must consider the source. Yes, I did respond in both of the above mentioned instances—but not in protest of what I thought I heard as a slight toward my child. My response was more in terms of what I thought each person meant. And in most cases, as I've stated, I am inclined toward either humor or nonchalance, especially when I am unsure about whether the comment actually merits anger.

When I was asked if my infant son had ever eaten a dog, it's true that my emotions came bubbling to the surface. It really did not matter whether this person was accepting of my son or not. My response was, "Of course not. He only has two teeth." And that ended the inquiry of what I assumed was the expression of a cruel untruth about my son's culture. However, while in Vietnam, I'd had my own suspicions about dog as part of the diet of the Vietnamese when I saw a litter of puppies standing on the corner outside a restaurant. But I quickly dismissed those thoughts. There was no way that I could wrap my Western brain around that concept. It took a long time, but at some point, I decided to do a little research about it—as I am wont to do in cases about which I want to get to the bottom of an issue. To my horror, it was true. The Vietnamese as well as other cultures do eat dog, some considering it to be quite a delicacy. Not only this, but it is a belief of the Vietnamese that the more an animal suffers before it is killed, the more tender will be the meat.

These facts may be what this man knows about Vietnamese culture. It was still wrong of him to take something that is anathema to American thinking and dump it on my son. But fortunately, this was the one and only comment I ever heard him make with regard to my son's heritage.

When Patrick called Lucas a "glasshoppa," I told him, "Just try to out-build Lucas with those Legos, and see what happens!" That said, I wanted to think on the comment a while longer. After all, the source of my initial discomfort with the word came from a child. Children are notorious for sometimes being rude or inappropriate. But children also learn things from the adults in their lives and from that which they are exposed to. I did not and still do not know in what context he learned this phrase said in just the way he said it. And curiously, I never heard him say it again after that. Perhaps he said it in front of his parents, and they corrected him. At any rate, it could be that had my son originated from my womb, he may have said the same thing.

I still think back fondly to the young grasshopper Caine and to the television series *Kung Fu*. I love that it was a time in which the social consciousness had been awakened to racism and discrimination of many cultures and that this show was a positive contribution to offenses endured by Asians dating back to the 1800s, when many were brought here to work at rail yards, virtually enslaved. Yet in nearly forty years how far have we actually come? In my estimation, with instances of highly visible celebrities slurring Asians (and there are a great deal more doing so than I have mentioned here) and of African-Americans still struggling to dispel myths about themselves and of angry, offensive people using social media to air their outrageous, provocative and completely discriminatory views of other races, not far enough.

Healing Questions

1. Do you feel that the media is responsible for perpetuating racism? What are some of your thoughts about highly visible people such as the ones mentioned mocking Asians?

2. Have you been unclear at times as to whether your child has actually been the recipient of a racial slight? How so?

3. Have you experienced any incidents of your child stereotyping or mocking his or her own race? How did this or would this make you feel? What might you do in response to such a situation?

16

Bow, Sweetie

John and I stood at the desk in the lobby of the Kim Do Hotel in Ho Chi Minh City, Vietnam. After weeks of having lived in that hotel waiting to receive our son, we finally had our baby in our arms—for keeps.

Only too thrilled to show him off, we propped him up on the counter for the hotel staff to see, and we folded him in half. "Bow, sweetie," I said to Lucas, offering the top of his head as a gesture of respect and good will toward the Vietnamese for this precious gift of a child. The staff smiled and commented on Lucas' good looks and on how lucky he was. Up and down our boy went, like a puppet bowing to a nightclub audience, as I repeated what I thought was a sign of respect through my child for his people.

Once home in the US, as we introduced our new son to family and friends, we did so with what we now considered a cute and cultural bow. I folded my baby in half so many times that it's a wonder he doesn't have a bad back.

As time went by and the introductions were all made, we stopped making Lucas perform the bow. We realized after a few months that what we had been imposing upon our son was a form of racial stereotyping. In effect, we were setting him apart as different from us, from our family and friends' children and from a culture in which bowing is not common. It no longer seemed cute. He was now a part of us, and in fact very early on our perception of him transformed a bit from this little Vietnamese baby from a strange and fascinating country to simply our child. It is true of a great number of parents who transracially adopt that when they see their kids, they don't see race. In fact, before we adopted Lucas I asked a mother of a Korean child what it was like to raise a daughter of a different race from hers. She replied that she didn't even really see her child as Korean but rather as "just my kid." There are many popular adoption quotes that express sentiments like, "I have four children. Two are adopted. I forget which two."

But a curious thing began to happen. As Lucas entered preschool, then kindergarten and beyond, he was sometimes approached and *asked* to bow. This mocking request mostly came from other children. In particular, I remember an unsettling and familiar scene in which Lucas was eight years old. At a small gathering of friends and family at my home, I happened to pass my son and another boy as they stood together near the kitchen. The other boy, hands pressed together while stiffly bowing, was speaking to my son in the derogatory "ching chong." Lucas stood silent, with his back to me, giving me no indication as to whether he felt hurt or annoyed. To my dismay, this was not the first time I had caught this other little boy speaking in this manner to my children.

Because I was hosting a party and did not want to embarrass anyone, I interrupted the offensive little display by asking the boys if they were hungry.

But it can be a tough call as to whether we as parents should address situations like these. My son at the time saw himself pretty much as a typical American kid. He may not have felt any offense in this reference to Asians. He never expressed to me that he had. If I had taken issue with this behavior by this boy and discussed it with Lucas, would I in essence have communicated to him that he is different from many of his friends and peers and that he should be hurt or offended by such conduct?

When is the time, since children seem to always grapple with "my agenda versus that of all those in authority over me," to add to this list of ongoing frustrations and issues of theirs racial injustice and the need to stand up to and defend against it?

What Hurts

My husband's and my thinking was skewed when we made Lucas bow. If we had given it any thought, we would have realized that the Vietnamese had not bowed to us while we were in their country. The repetitive action we imposed upon our son was not reciprocal but some sort of stereotype we brought with us to Vietnam that we assumed to be appropriate. Besides, no one there or in this country expects an infant to understand or to communicate such an expression of capitulation to an adult. We as adults are meant to yield to our children's needs and feelings and teach them to respect us, over time, in a manner that is suitable to our cultural and personal systems and beliefs as our children develop a basic comprehension of the meaning of respect.

Bowing was neither a preservation of Lucas' cultural heritage nor was it an appropriate gesture to make him perform for our friends and family. The action reeks of submission and subservience, implying, "You are superior—therefore I stoop before you."

Unfortunately, sometimes what goes around comes around. Since those early days of forcing my son to bow, I now find it disturbing indeed when other children try to engage my children in this action—especially in conjunction with the expression of "ching chong." Just as my husband and I once did, they associate the performance of such behavior with my children because my kids are of Asian heritage.

Ignorant children and adults, through varying forms of what they are exposed to and the ways in which they have interpreted stereotyping as acceptable, mimic aspects of a widespread, all-too-often tolerated caricature of a large population that is growing increasingly tired of how it has been portrayed for years. Even within the evangelical church, a place in which we are supposed to feel inclusiveness as one body and where racial reconciliation has in fact been pursued, Asians still feel disillusioned and frustrated.

According to "An Open Letter from the Asian American Community to the Evangelical Church," written by Asian American Christians United and signed by hundreds, the sentiment among Asian-Americans is that this "segment of the church continues to be misunderstood, misrepresented, and misjudged." They cite several instances of racism within the church that have caught the public's eye in recent years but believe that there are really hundreds more that have actually occurred.[1]

It can be said that the catalyst for the letter began with a Facebook post by Pastor Rick Warren, the bestselling author of *The Purpose Driven Life* and pastor of Orange County, California-based Saddleback Church.

After he returned from opening the church's Hong Kong campus in September 2013, Warren posted a photograph of a Red Guard, the young Communist cadres that policed their communities during Mao Zedong's Cultural Revolution. It depicted a smiling, red-cheeked young woman dressed in the drab gray uniform that the Red Guard typically wore. The post said, "The typical attitude of Saddleback Staff as they start work each day."[2]

In an article for National Public Radio's Code Switch, author Karen Grigsby Bates explains why this offended many Asian Christians: "Many come from Chinese immigrant families, some of which suffered greatly during Mao's Great Leap Forward and the Cultural Revolution that followed. (More than 15 million people are estimated to have died during that Great Leap, from 'discipline' administered by the Red Army and from outright starvation, the product of nonsensical agricultural practices that, literally, bore no fruit.)"[3]

Warren initially laughed off the attention that his post received. A few weeks later he spoke at a conference in which a video was used to show a pastor working with his intern. Meant to be a learning tool, the video portrayed a white pastor talking in a fake Asian accent engaging in goofy karate with another character, lots of bowing and tinny "Asian" music playing in the background.[4] This incident on the heels of Warren's previous insensitivity to the Asian community was more than it could bear, and thus the open letter's creation and circulation.

In addition to these highly publicized incidents, the letter adds that VBS curriculum, youth skits and general trade books have also done harm to Asians in that they have "been caricatured, mocked, or otherwise treated as foreigners outside the typical accepted realm of white evangelicalism."[5]

Grace Given

Many of us might wish that our children—particularly those whom we internationally adopt—came with a manual, which of course they don't. John and I found ourselves not only thrust into parenthood with a ten-month-old but with a foreign-born baby whose culture—with its vast differences from ours, its complexity and its difficult history—we struggled to understand. We were naïve, excited and overwhelmed all at once. Not a good mix for producing the clearest and wisest of thinking.

But we had to afford ourselves some grace and forgive ourselves for all that early bowing of our son. As first-time parents to a foreign-born adopted son, we never meant any harm. We soon realized the error of our ways and repented, asking forgiveness from God for stereotyping our son and turning away from such behavior.

I admit that some of the mistakes I have made in this whole process have been the result of ignorance. "Ignorant" is a word that *The American Heritage Dictionary of the English Language* describes as "showing or arising from a lack of education or knowledge" and that of being "unaware or uninformed."[6] While ignorance is greatly frowned upon by many, it is not a sin. Human beings are not omniscient creatures; we do not run our lives with the ability to engage in any and every situation with complete and accurate information and sensitivity. To do so is simply not realistic. Expression of our ignorance may actually result in a learning process or heightened awareness of truth—if we are willing to learn.

We must extend grace and forgiveness to those who have not learned. This is especially true when it originates from children who have been influenced by things such as racist VBS skits or other means in which Asians have been caricatured and mocked.

When it comes to intelligent, visible and influential people in our society who "ought to know better" and to the church, where of all places we expect unity and acceptance, it has to be with a great deal of difficulty that the distraught Asian-American population can offer grace. How does an ethnic group that feels it has endured an endless onslaught of cultural insensitivity, racial stereotyping and mere tokenism from those who profess to love others with the love of Christ forgive?

One way to afford grace is to recognize that racial stereotyping is not limited to people of the majority race in a culture. Not long ago, when my son and his friend were at a neighborhood park, they were confronted by a group of minority children (whose particular ethnicity is really irrelevant in this case). While minorities themselves, and quite possibly having felt the pain of prejudice at some time, they decided to try to incite my son with racial slurs against his Asian background. I found this both curious and upsetting.

As we live in an increasingly diverse society and as transracial families and multiethnic communities become more and more common, we must be increasingly cautious about lumping together all members of a race into a single category. This goes both directions. As a parent of Asian-American children, I would never be a person who demeans Asian-Americans .

Another way to offer grace, which I'll state yet again, is to consider the source. The church is comprised of sinners of all kinds. Leadership is no exception. Everyone within the body of Christ is in a different place, each of us multifaceted, complex individuals in our spiritual journeys. Some are brand-new Christians, carrying years of baggage from lives that were not turned over to God for a long time. Still others have become complacent in their Christian lives or highly distracted by and overly involved in works and ministries.

And, as I stated in chapter 13, we often expect much more love, sensitivity and Christlike behavior from our Christian brothers and sisters than we do from nonbelievers. In my unique position as a Christian mother to children of Asian descent, I was disturbed by what I read in the open letter, and I saw it as justified. But I also recognize that the church is a place in which we make ourselves vulnerable as we connect with others in the body of Christ. It's this vulnerability and our sometimes high expectations that frequently cause us disappointment and hurt in the place we least expect it. We need to curb our expectations of the church and to recognize that as we regularly attend, we are intertwining our lives with others and working with broken, wounded, sinful, hurting, struggling and ignorant people like ourselves who are on a journey to wholeness and transformation.

We should also recognize that some racism is inadvertent and unintentional. Many do not set out to malign other ethnicities on purpose. Being exposed to racist views throughout a lifetime or becoming a Christian later in life can be the source of insensitivity to other cultures. Also a sin issue such as one's own ethnic pride or even fear of other races can lead to racism. As the evangelical church has become less "white" over time, it is not surprising that a number of minority groups have had to struggle with issues they feel exclude or demean their particular races.

I am certainly not an expert on racism. I am simply trying to present varying sentiments on a rather complicated issue. Sadly, we see how far we've yet to go in our culture and as followers of Christ to create an atmosphere of racial harmony and respect for all peoples. In all situations a measure of grace must be afforded. We all must be "quick to hear" and "slow to speak" (James 1:19), as the Bible commands us, considering how our words and actions may affect others. Yet we are called to forgive, as painful a process as that may be for some who have valid reasons for anger and disapproval. God's Word tells us that if we do not forgive others for their transgressions, neither will we be forgiven. But that doesn't mean that confrontation isn't sometimes necessary to bring about reconciliation or that true reconciliation happens overnight.

And it is important to note that forgiveness and reconciliation are not the same exact things. While to forgive an offense is to pardon a person from it, reconciliation involves more of a relational aspect. When we are truly reconciled with someone who has hurt us, we reestablish a balance or harmony in our relationship with that individual.

Handling It

In fact, God encourages us to go to our brother when he has sinned against us. I believe it is God's desire for us to address an offense committed against us by another party in a prompt fashion so that bitterness won't take root within us. In some cases, when I have experienced short encounters with strangers, I have not always been able to go to an offending party and express my hurt. Sometimes I have had to evaluate whether or not I was actually being hurt. However, there have been instances in which I should have approached a brother or sister in Christ and shared with that person how what he or she said or did hurt me or my kids. And there have been times when I should have stepped out to someone I have offended and asked for forgiveness for my words or actions. But I am a work in progress who dearly dislikes confrontation. Through my experiences as an adoptive parent to internationally born children, God has shown me more about these issues and how I must work on them. For that I am thankful.

As I have discussed throughout this book, others' ignorance can be countered with teaching moments in which we can respond to them with a calm demeanor or with the biblically sound soft answer (see Prov. 15:1). People always seem to be more tolerant of hearing something when it is presented in a nonthreatening, non-judgmental fashion. No one likes to be called ignorant, even if he or she is, and using a person's inappropriate comment to educate, enlighten or even inspire in a positive way is always possible.

On the other hand, when it is we whose actions or words may not be the result of the wisest of choices in a given situation, we can always ask God for wisdom, because His Word says that to anyone who asks for wisdom, He will give it generously (see James 1:5).

But first we have to come to the conclusion that we regularly need wisdom from God, and we need to take heed to those little "checks" in our spirit and allow the Holy Spirit to convict us about a situation. Completely distracted with my new son, I did not incorporate these principles into my role of motherhood as I forced my baby to bow. But I am glad that making him do so soon became uncomfortable to me. Perhaps the Lord was speaking to my heart about a part of my parenting that did not please Him and was not respectful to my child. Being busy and distracted with a thousand things to do is one of the means by which the Enemy seeks to drown out the voice of God and the conviction of the Holy Spirit in our hearts.

While there are ways in which we can handle hurtful racist comments, I do think two things. First, if we look for racism, we are bound to find it. And second, that is because God never promised us utopia on earth. Some element of racism will likely always prevail until Jesus returns and creates perfection for us to live in. We have to face the fact that not everyone is willing to become a godly person. Toward these kinds of people we do feel a sense of righteous indignation for their callousness and their refusal to stop perpetuating stereotypes. These people are lost. We can pray for them or, if we are the offended party, communicate to them the kind of effect they have on others.

My kids usually don't identify others by race, color or creed. They don't even identify people of their own races as "one of the other Chinese girls in class" or "the Asian store owner down the block." And I don't use racial references when I refer to others. Rather, I find something unique and positive about another individual that does not draw any attention to their particular ethnicity such as "the little girl in your class who draws beautiful rainbows" or "your funny aunt."

I certainly hope that my children will always know that they can trust me to talk about any of the ways they feel slighted or violated by others due to racial prejudice. As things have come up, we have had discussions about them. This can be uncomfortable for us, but it's important as adoptive parents to foreign-born children to keep the dialogue going.

Healing Questions

1. If you are part of a transracial family, have you ever stereotyped your child? How so?

2. Have other children or adults made racial references about your child? If so, how have you responded to such comments and questions?

3. Is there a good time for you to bring up racial differences with your child? If so, when?

17

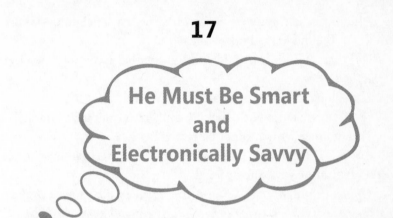

He Must Be Smart and Electronically Savvy

A trip to Grandma's house is special for our family. There is always a feast simmering on the stove in anticipation of our arrival. My mom knows just how to greet us with a broad smile and with heartfelt hugs and kisses as though we are her favorite people in the entire world. And does she ever love the grandchildren! It is rare indeed when she hasn't picked up a toy or a gift for one of her grandkids "just because."

After a walk through town, usually to a nearby harbor and park, she'll sit on a bench with her back to the wind and water, and she'll sun herself as Lucas tears the place up. After a couple hours of swings and sailboats, monkey bars and mayhem, we're ready to head back to her place for all the wonderful culinary delights she has whipped up.

Hand in hand she and Lucas walked on a bright, sunny Saturday afternoon. He, three; she, seventy years older; youth and wisdom side by side, two of my favorite people on earth strolling through town. It warmed my heart.

"Marilyn!" a voice rang out.

We all turned to see who had called my mother.

"Oh gawsh, what'a you doin' here?" asked a woman, mid-seventies, thick glasses and heavy pink lipstick.

"My daughter, son-in-law and grandson are in town for a visit," replied my mother.

After introductions were made with Thelma, a neighbor of my mother's, Thelma looked down at Lucas.

"Hi there, honey," she said and brought her face way down to Lucas' level.

Lucas looked at her and stared.

"You's sure a cutie pie," Thelma said. "He's oriental. Chinese?"

"Vietnamese," my mother corrected her.

"Well," Thelma said, "he's Asian, right? He must be smart and electrawnically savvy," she decided.

Oh no, I thought. *Here we go again. How am I to respond to this woman who is embarrassing herself and stereotyping my son but apparently clueless as to how she is accomplishing either?*

My son *is* smart and electronically savvy. But so are millions of other kids of all nationalities. In today's information age that is filled with so many technological toys, gadgets and games, what kid *doesn't* pick up on it all?

Computers are to Lucas' generation what the library and encyclopedias were to mine, but they offer lightning speed and greater thoroughness in transference of information from fingertips to brain to assignment page.

In part due to technology but also because of numerous changes in child rearing over the years, kids today are smarter and savvier than children of years ago. For instance, I never went to preschool. Doing so just wasn't the norm when I was a kid. But today it is not only a standard but even a necessary experience for children at the ages of three and four in order for them to be on par with other five-year-olds when they enter kindergarten. If children are found not to be up to group performance with their peers, a wide array of state-funded interventions are available to them that cover everything from learning challenges to physical disabilities. Educational books, programs and games are a multibillion dollar industry.

We also discuss more things with our children today than parents did years ago. I have had to learn from wiser parents than I and through trial and error how to handle questions such as "Where do babies come from?" and to offer my kids a better answer than I received: "The stork." As for "Why does Frank have two dads and not a mom?" this was something we never heard of in the seventies and eighties. If I had ever asked my parents that question, I'd probably have been told, "Frank lives with his dad and his *uncle*."

We also talk to our children today about their feelings, and we encourage them to express their emotions. This was not a popular child-rearing technique a generation or so ago. From parents to teachers to clergy, nobody ever asked me or my siblings how we felt about anything. But today it's all about "How does that make you feel?" and "It seems as if you're feeling angry" or "That must have made you feel awful." All this draws kids out of themselves, prompts communication and gives them a better understanding of themselves and of those around them. It makes them smarter about not only their own emotions but those of others.

What Hurts

Why are so many Asian-Americans presumed to be Chinese? From my experience, when non-Asians encounter Asian-Americans, the first thing that comes to people's minds is that they must be Chinese. This is both curious and a bit annoying, as I've heard my son referred to as Chinese many times over the course of his lifetime. "China man," and words drawn from "ching chong" imposed upon him make it seem that a lot of people have no idea about the world they live in and just how many Asian cultures exist outside of China. I have thought a time or two, *Hey, if you're going to draw attention to the racial difference between my son and that of yourself as well as of his parents, at least get a clue as to what that difference might be.* I don't know to what extent other Asian-Americans not of Chinese descent come across this generalization. However, I've heard people I've encountered refer to Asians with statements such as, "I don't know what he is, Chinese or Korean or something." Why must the people spoken about be discussed with regard to their race as Asians at all?

And of course, there it was in Thelma's words staring me in the face again—that word "oriental." I've already discussed why this particular label is offensive. And to boot, the assumption about my three-year-old's interests and abilities. One, two, three jabs in less than a minute of meeting this woman.

Lucas is not gifted because of his ethnicity but because he was designed by God. The Lord is the One who knit him together (see Ps. 139:13) in his biological mother's womb and knew all his days "before one of them came to be" (139:16 NIV). It is God who gave him his talents, gifts and abilities so that they may be used by Lucas for the good that God has for him to do.

This isn't to say that what we are good at shouldn't be used for our enjoyment or for a sense of personal accomplishment.

In the movie *Chariots of Fire*, Eric Liddell, a gifted runner, refused to race on Sundays because as a Christian, he honored this day that God has set apart as a holy day of Sabbath rest. Still, of his athletic ability he said, "When I run, I feel God's pleasure."

When we do what God has gifted us to do with pure motives and in the manner in which God desires for us, it can be exhilarating. Of course we experience joy and fun and excitement when we do these things. But to say that my child must be smart and electronically savvy because he is Asian singles him out as different from other children because of his race. Besides, how many of us parents of any race have sighed in resignation over an electronics issue and asked one of our kids to help us?

As adoptive parents to children of different ethnic backgrounds than ours, my husband and I are sometimes concerned that they will mythologize themselves based on their cultures. No longer that innocent three-year-old but now a preadolescent and an honor-roll student, Lucas recently told my husband and me, "I'm smart because I'm Asian." I don't think he woke up one morning having come to that conclusion on his own. He must have heard someone refer to Asians as smart—another deeply ingrained cultural myth. We told him that he is a God-gifted intelligent boy not based on his ethnicity. We explained that by believing the statement he had made he is actually stereotyping himself. We asked him, "What about your friends at school who are just as smart as you or maybe even smarter? Are they of Asian descent as well?" He had to admit that smart kids in school are from various ethnic backgrounds.

And, we also pointed out to him, being careful not to make him feel superior, that although it's true that he never seems to open a book or have the need to study, he lives with a perfect example of how the assumption is untrue: "What about your sister? While she is smart too, she has to work hard at getting good grades, and she too is Asian." I think we got the point across to him.

Grace Given

It has been suggested that my child is a whiz in the making because of his handle on electronics and computers and such. I give grace to those who say this, in particular to those who are in their senior years. As I have mentioned, the older we are, the more likely we are to have developed stereotypes and judgments about others based on race. I also think that the exponential increase in technological advances that people who grew up during the Depression Era have seen must be a bit mindboggling.

To remember that people like Thelma grew up listening to static-filled radio programs for entertainment, not owning a television set and having to "walk five miles to school, barefoot in the snow, carrying a cold potato for lunch" allows me to offer this grace.

I also admit that my husband and I are not the most technologically savvy people on the planet either. We pale in comparison to an average eight-year-old when it comes to our electronic expertise. For instance, I never programmed a VCR in the days before

DVD players became standard, and any minor problem with my computer leaves me at the mercy of a geek squad or my son for expertise and guidance.

But Lucas does figure this stuff out much more easily than I do. For one thing, I think there is a bit of sequential understanding that goes on for kids today. The result of using one piece of technology creates a feel for that item, which leads to an increased understanding for other devices and the way in which they work. It's sort of like acquiring language skills.

It is said that the best time for a person to learn new languages is when they are quite young. Little ones soak up languages with relative ease. By the time we reach our thirties or forties, however, it's a lot more difficult for us to learn another language. The same applies to technology. If people are exposed to it in their early years, they can get a much better handle on it.

I also choose to give grace to those who have an image in their minds of smart and successful Asian children and adults. And admittedly, it does help in the grace-giving department when I hear something good about my child, sometimes even when it is a stereotype. I like people to recognize my son's intelligence, skills and abilities.

There is some truth in our image of the intelligent, professional Asian person. In many Asian cultures there is a high standard of excellence that children are expected to achieve. I grew up in a suburb of New York in which the only Asians I knew were upper-middle class with white-collar jobs.

In some Asian countries, a strong foundation for children is laid of discipline, hard work and success, and this is not just for the child and the family's sake. These countries see this as a means of enabling the nation to succeed and to progress and compete on a global level.

Handling It

I cannot say for certain, of course, exactly which traits have been passed on to my children through their genes. Many children grow up having completely different interests and abilities than their biological parents, and the opposite is sometimes true as well.

We've all heard expressions such as "He's a chip off the old block" and "The apple doesn't fall far from the tree." And there are families in which generations of children grow up to follow in their ancestors' footsteps in career choice. But I do believe that there has to be a difference between a family's genes and an entire nation's genes. Otherwise, even when I hear a positive, albeit sideways, compliment about my son, it still feels too much as if I'm hearing something like "All Irish are drunks" or "Germans are cold and stoic people" or "All Italians are loud and expressive," all things I've heard with reference to John's and my mixed heritages. These are unfair generalizations.

I thank people who praise my son, but I do not encourage the stereotyping of "his" people. If others make a complimentary comment in front of him, I am usually quick to point out that God has made him special in many different ways, not just in his intelligence or his electronic savvy. Lucas is also funny and sociable, tender and compassionate.

So there I stood with the dear old presumptuous Thelma. I knew that she meant no ill will, and we had already corrected her on Lucas' race. I suppose that it was out of respect for my mother, and of not wanting to cause any hurt feelings or anger in Thelma that might affect future interactions with my mom, that I didn't say what I really wanted to. I didn't tell her, "I know you mean well, but you've made three racist remarks about my son. Let me explain how." No, I simply told Thelma, "Lucas is a blessing and into so many different things." Not every encounter like this is a teaching moment. In this case I thought that to correct my mom's friend would have caused more harm than good, embarrassed my mother and likely not have been received well by Thelma.

But it's OK. I know in my heart, and I want Lucas and Olivia to discover in theirs too, that the greatest traits we can have are those that honor God and demonstrate to others that we are of godly character.

Ultimately, what being a parent to my children of Asian heritage has taught me so far—and I'm always learning as I continue as a parent—is that I have had my own preconceived notions, assumptions and stereotypes about everything from infertility to my children's cultures. I have had to own up to that.

Also, though I've experienced hurtful comments and questions throughout my journey to motherhood and beyond, some may consider my experiences tame compared to what they may have experienced and what really exists out there by way of prejudice. Others may have dealt with less in their situations.

While I or my children have been the recipients of everything I've written about, I consider myself and my children fortunate. My family has for the most part experienced acceptance by our loved ones, friends, community, church members and those at my children's schools. Apart from the incident in the park in which children of another minority mocked Lucas, I've never heard my kids mention that they've been called any horrible words that are used to discriminate against Asians, nor have they expressed to me that they have ever felt out of place or rejected by their peers due to their race. And, thank God, nobody has ever tried to intimidate and hurt my children with any type of physical assault. We do live in New York, in the United States, a place that one of our pastors, an Asian, describes as "one of the most diverse, tolerant and accepting places on earth." For all this, I am thankful.

Yet I know that real racism exists. While I have done what I can to protect and defend my children against it, albeit bungling my way through it all sometimes, I have my concerns. As my children grow and are exposed to more news, more social media, more people and cultures, will they develop a more heightened awareness of discrimination toward Asians? How will this affect them?

It was with great dismay that my husband recently informed me that he overheard Lucas on the phone with a Chinese-American friend of his, both making jokes about none other than Asians. While my husband did address this and have a conversation with Lucas about the discriminatory nature of his jokes and ask him why he would poke fun at his own and his friend's races, Lucas didn't have a lot to say. To me, this indicates perhaps a deeper issue going on with him about his cultural heritage. Yet it is difficult to draw much information from a twelve-year-old about his feelings.

At the same time, I do think it necessary to find an appropriate venue for my son to communicate some of what may be stirring around in that very nearly adolescent head of his. There are counselors, culture camps and adult Asian friends of ours whom we can draw upon for support and guidance. We want Lucas to fully accept himself for who he is and where he came from while treating other ethnicities with respect and acceptance.

All this makes me want to keep my finger on the pulse of anti-racial sentiment and hate in this country. As parents who are part of a transracial family, that isn't a bad thing. We also have the added task of talking about race, in particular their own races, with our children, as uncomfortable as that might seem sometimes. It is a process—protecting our kids, helping them accept themselves and others, dealing with their sense of abandonment as infants, helping them find their way in a world that can often be cruel and unfair. But we owe it to them. Most of all we owe them God's perspective on all this. God hates discrimination, for after all, His word says that he is "no respecter of persons" (Acts 10:34, KJV; see also James 2:1). He loves all of us.

Healing Questions

1. Has your child ever been stereotyped in a positive way due to his or her ethnic background? In what way?

2. What has been or would be your response to such an occurrence?

3. What are some stereotypes that have truth contained in them?

PART 4

Don't Say It to the Parents

18

You're Such Good People for Adopting!

The day of my baby shower had arrived. I had been to a hundred showers in years past, but now it was finally my turn to celebrate the impending arrival of the baby that would soon be in my arms.

As I went to take my seat in my special chair of honor, one of the guests walked up to me and grabbed my arm. She planted herself toe to toe with me so that I could smell the Chardonnay she had consumed earlier while she had mingled with the guests.

"You're such good people for adopting," she said to me. I just looked at her and smiled. She then launched into a spiel about how wonderful my husband and I were to start a family in this way.

It wasn't the first time I had heard this, nor would it be the last. I have had my perceived virtues extolled for what has seemed hours until I have appeared on par with the likes of Mother Teresa in the eyes of my admirers.

What Hurts

I wanted a child. I couldn't conceive a child. Reproductive technologies did not work to create in me a child. The domestic adoption route proved difficult. So God intervened and brought a child into our lives to love and raise from across the globe. God, not me.

It's uncomfortable and unnerving to be told how wonderful you are to adopt. Apart from this, it's not really true.

Couples have different motives for adopting. One couple my husband and I met in China had already raised three children, the youngest of whom was in her thirties. Despite being well into their fifties, they felt led to start a new adopted family and were about to pick up their second adopted daughter. They seemed like wonderful people, but no one in the group elevated them to sainthood. In fact, I remember thinking at the time that it seemed a little crazy for them to be taking on such responsibility at their age.

Then of course there were Cathy and Jarrod, whom I mentioned previously, with Cathy unable to fly to China for their adopted baby in her third trimester of pregnancy. Instead, Jarrod's mother accompanied Jarrod in picking up his and Cathy's daughter. Jarrod and Cathy seemed to be a great couple, taking on a biological new-born and a newly adopted one-year-old at the same time. Before I got to know them, I wondered if Cathy had been surprised with a pregnancy after she and her husband had already begun the adoption process for China. Perhaps she was one of those who was told after deciding to adopt, "Now you'll get pregnant!" and it really happened for her.

But we need not extol people's virtues. Whatever their stories, adoptive couples are pretty much average people who just desire a child—or another child. Then there is me. First told that I was too selfish to have children and then told by an aunt that it was selfish not to have children, I felt sometimes that my overwhelming need to have a baby was selfish.

I wanted what I saw everyone around me enjoying—a soft bundle in my arms who would gaze up at me with a contented, peaceful look on his or her face. I wanted those gooey, wet kisses, toothless smiles and sweet laughter from this little person for whom I could open up the world and a world of possibilities. I wanted to be like my five sisters and my brother, all of whom had kids, and like those in my church family, who just kept on bringing more little souls into the kingdom, and like just about every aunt, cousin and niece in my family who were raising families. Me, such a good person for adopting? I didn't think so at all.

Grace Given

I give grace to the "gushers" because I realize that those who tell my husband and me what good people we are for adopting don't actually consider us the next best thing to sliced bread. But somehow, through the adoptions of our children, we've risen from the ranks of those of good character, moral responsibility and even selflessness to some elevated status of sainthood.

I know that many of these people love us and loved us well before we adopted. I believe that they are genuine in their admiration for a couple's decision to travel to a foreign country where they will receive a little stranger into their arms and commit to that child for life. They may have thought about adoption as an option for themselves at one time, or perhaps they feel a great sense of compassion for orphaned children who live in poverty throughout the world and are thankful when they see some of these children being given homes and families and futures.

OK, maybe we're a little bit good to go through the process of adoption. That's because for those who adopt because they cannot bear biological children, there exists in many of our hearts a deep sense of injustice.

While we read about yet another baby dumped in the trash, we leap through hurdles to qualify as parents. We fill out form after form, submit to criminal background checks, sit through interviews and counsel and sometimes end up on the receiving end of the worst kinds of outrageous behavior and comments.

For instance, my husband and I were required to take blood tests at our local health department in order to be screened for HIV AIDS before we could adopt our son Lucas.

I didn't mind the test. I knew that taking it was necessary so that an orphan would not be given a new home with a parent who had AIDS. It was what came after the test that offended me—and after that, and after that . . .

Even though we were in our late thirties and had been married for three years, John and I were subjected to a required counseling session on "safe sex" practices. We listened politely to this misdirected sermon to a monogamous, married Christian couple. After all, in every way an adoptive couple worries about being offensive to any party who may have influence over their ultimate goal of getting their baby.

Our "counsel" complete, we rose to leave the office, but not before being handed a condom. This pouring of salt into my still raw infertility wounds would have enraged me had it not been so ludicrous. Our counselor knew why we were there. Was this, I wondered, the equivalent of being handed a lollipop at the doctor's office for being a good patient?

When I stared at the prophylactic in my hand as though it were a red-hot lump of coal, the social worker smiled and said, "Our parting gift to you. It's part of our protocol."

I exited that building a little shook up but relieved too that I could check another thing off our adoption to-do list. But then we passed a car in the almost empty parking lot. In that hunk of metal that sat and absorbed the June sun, we saw two small children. A young girl of about three or four years of age sat in the back seat next to a baby strapped in a car seat. I peered through the open windows but saw no parent in the car. Then I scanned the parking lot only to realize that my husband and I were the only adults outside the building.

To find small children unattended in a hot car, after being forced to give blood and leave the health department with a condom because I wanted my own baby, created an even greater sense of injustice in my world. I can tell you that it was mighty difficult for me that day to deal with my anger toward all the irresponsible, fertile people in the world.

That night as I tossed and turned in bed, I couldn't stop asking God, whom I know is loving and just, why those children's parents were able to conceive and I was not. I would never leave a child alone in a car.

Handling It

So often we judge people for their deeds rather than their character, or we assume their deeds reflect a magnificent character. We look at someone who gives away large sums of money to charities and assume that he or she is such a good, giving person. Yet we are unaware that that person is miserly with his or her own children's needs or constantly nags a spouse for spending money on household essentials.

We see that member of our church who seems to flawlessly head up multiple ministries and think of him or her as such a fruitful Christian whom we wish we could be like. Meanwhile, we don't recognize that hidden within a part of that person's character is a need for control and attention and that the person enjoys all the distraction that actually keeps him or her from being in close fellowship with the Lord.

And how often do we hear people applaud others for getting into good schools, holding down important, high-paying jobs or being elected to public offices? Much of the time. What we don't hear is how some of these smart, high achievers spend their personal time poring over pornography sites, excessively drinking or failing to deliver on promises they have made.

Corruption and deception run rampant in the culture in which we live. Beneath some man who coaches young boys in baseball lies a child predator. Within some cop who protects and serves his city is a drug-addicted man who buys his illegal substance of choice from the very people he knows should be off the streets. Underneath a charismatic personality, crisp Armani suit and smooth voice exists a politician who accepts bribes and does more harm than good to his constituents who have counted on him to bring about positive changes that do not materialize.

How often have we heard people exclaim with genuine surprise, "I would never have expected her to do something like that," or, "I didn't think he had that in him." The media provides an endless saga of the terrible things people do to the completely unsuspecting around them. "But he was so good with the kids," they'll say, or, "She was such a caring nurse—how could she murder her patients?"

But God is impressed by none of our images or the seemingly charitable things that we do. Not when they spring out of impure motives, are used to impress or are offered by those who stray from Him. In this case God says that our works to Him are like "filthy rags" (Isa. 64:6 NIV).

I'm certainly not suggesting that all adoptive parents are hiding serious character defects and sin. I'm simply making an observation that a lot of people make judgments based on the appearance of things. But God looks at the heart. And while we should look for the good in others, for that is how we elevate them to their true potential, we should also explore people's characters, because that is what is indicative of who they truly are. Please don't tell me that I'm a good person for adopting. You don't know my story or my heart or how I parent, nor do you know some of the mistakes I make.

Was the woman who drowned her little adopted boy because she could not handle his troublesome behavior so good for adopting? Or how about another woman who adopted a son from Russia and then, when he was around seven years old, made the awful decision to put him on a plane alone and send him back to his birth country? Was she good for perpetuating an international scandal and causing the Russians to shut down adoptions? Or, more importantly, for leaving a little boy with a trauma and a rejection that he will likely always remember?

Take Cathy and Jarrod. I highly doubt that they would say that they are good people for adopting their Chinese daughter as they almost simultaneously experienced the birth of their biological son. Based on their struggles to split their time and attention between two new children and the fact that Chase's birth overshadowed their daughter's arrival into their lives by others' behavior, I think that they must have had their moments when they wondered, "What have we gotten ourselves into?"

I struggled in those early days after bringing home my son, sometimes desperate in my awkward attempts to figure out how to be a mother to a baby who had already developed a little personality, preferences, habits and expectations from caregivers. Was I a good person for adopting when my husband arrived home from work to find me sitting in a chair in the living room, overwhelmed and sobbing in frustration?

Or how about those endless nights that we experienced for years when my daughter would cry in the middle of the night and I just didn't want to get out of bed? Did my irritation and lack of understanding over this ongoing suffering of hers make me a good person? Or did hearing the voice of the Enemy saying "Some people can't have children because they shouldn't" and believing it make me good?

Those who have biological children as well as those who adopt are mere human beings who mostly try as best they can to meet the challenges and struggles of parenthood. Yet I never hear birth parents told, "You are so good for procreating!"

I am also aware that there are groups of people out there who are vigorously opposed to the fact that my husband and I have internationally adopted. They cite reasons for their disapproval that range from corruption in international adoption practices to women being forced to relinquish their children or having them stolen to trauma being inflicted on children who will resent being adopted by people of races other than their own and "ripped" from their native land, culture and heritage to the fact that there are so many children in our own country that are in need of adoption.

They raise some valid points that the people who have told us how good we are for adopting our children may likely not be aware of.

My children have experienced some issues with regard to international adoption: racism, my daughter's dismay over her biological mother "not wanting" her, my son's curiosity about how much he cost as well as the sadness he has felt whenever I have mentioned the orphanage he lived in. I cannot know exactly how they will feel as they grow and mature about the choices that have been made for them in terms of being given up by their biological parents and brought to the United States by my husband and me to raise them.

Throughout my work on this book, I have been afforded the opportunity through God, who reconciles us with others and Himself, to go back to people I have discussed within these pages. I have been able to express to them that something said long ago hurt me or to ask forgiveness of them for an ignorant, hurtful comment I made. God is amazing to me in that He has brought about all these conversations to further heal my heart and perhaps to give others the chance to let go of unforgiveness toward me. But the glaring reality is that my children won't likely be able to have these types of healing, reconciliatory interactions with the people who brought them into this world and then gave them up.

What I do know is that a part of me has been glad to be included among those who comprise a bigger picture: to be one who has had the privilege of removing children from lives in which they potentially would not have known the love of parents, of extended families and of God and of being able to give them opportunities other than garbage picking or prostitution. Another part of me has had my somewhat needy, envious, selfish desires to become a mother fulfilled. Neither makes me a good person nor a bad one. I am merely a fallible one, capable of sin and mistakes that God—who dearly loves me—forgives while He helps me mature and grow in Him. The same can be said for parents to biological children as well.

My husband and I insist to those who applaud us that our children are the ones who bless us because they give us so much. We want people to walk away from this book with the message that God put these children into our arms, and for that our hearts and lives are so much fuller. I didn't become a better person for having adopted. Having children makes me a better person, because God uses our kids to mold us and shape us more into the image of Christ—if we allow Him to. That goes for anybody's children.

Healing Questions

1. What good things have people said about you for having adopted?

2. What has been your response to such statements?

3. How easy or difficult was the process of adopting your child?

19

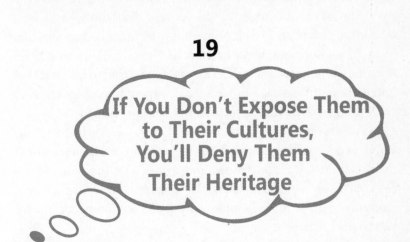

If You Don't Expose Them to Their Cultures, You'll Deny Them Their Heritage

Iknew two women who each adopted a child from Asia. Karen has a little girl whose culture she has invested much time and energy to incorporate into her family's everyday lives. She has a special ethnic dish in honor of her child's heritage on her table at every dinner. She often dresses her daughter in the traditional garb of her native country and takes pictures of her in these outfits and then mails these photos to family and friends at Christmas. She also celebrates Asian holidays on a regular basis and has kept her daughter's given Asian name.

This little girl, without prompting from any adult, has always expressed a deep gratitude for her adoption, though she was just an infant when she came to this country with Karen and her husband.

My other friend, Lisa, has a son and doesn't do any of these kinds of things. She and the rest of her family, including a biological daughter, are Irish. She considers her adopted Vietnamese son Irish now as well. He lives in New York and has been assimilated into that culture, and Lisa will tell you that that's that.

I have compared both friends' approaches to parenting internationally adopted children, and I have to say that I admired Karen's enthusiasm to experience her daughter's culture with her as she grew up. I wanted to do that with Lucas as well, and I thought it would be a great disservice to him not to draw his own culture into our lives. When Lucas was little, I dreamed of how I would spend hours learning to cook traditional Vietnamese foods, read to him stacks of books about his heritage and otherwise expose him to a wide array of all things Asian. That is, until things began to go a little haywire.

One afternoon my husband and I took a then-two-year-old Lucas to a Vietnamese exhibit at the Museum of Natural History in New York City. We clapped and smiled and brought his tiny face up close to the plastic-encased apparel and artifacts in our attempts to make for him some kind of connection between what he saw and who he is.

Lucas, a naturally exuberant baby, seemed rather unimpressed by the whole lot of cultural goodies. In my naiveté and overzealousness, I felt a twinge of disappointment. *Oh well*, I thought, *he will love the highlight of the exhibit for sure.* This included a traditional dragon dance in which a long papier-mâché replica of the dragon in fiery reds, intense oranges and blinding yellows seemed to float from one end of the large lobby outside the exhibit area to the other. My husband and I thought this would be quite meaningful for Lucas, since the name given to him by his birthmother, "Long," means "dragon." But once again, even in the midst of this fantastic display, Lucas' face appeared rather expressionless.

That is, until later on that night. When I put Lucas down to sleep in his crib, he clutched at the bars and refused to lie down. He stared up at me with wide, fear-filled eyes. Frightened by his behavior, I tried to lift him up, but I couldn't loosen his grip on the crib. "Lucas, what's wrong?" I asked.

"I 'cared of the dragon, Mommy, I 'cared," he said.

My earlier disappointment at Lucas' apparent lack of interest in the Vietnamese displays morphed immediately into shame. I realized that in my unbridled passion to expose my two-year-old to his heritage, and through a lack of wisdom in assuming that he would be inherently drawn to it, I had frightened my baby. For years after that, the boy who had been named "Dragon" expressed fear of the creatures.

So I began to show him DVDs of our trip to Vietnam, but within two minutes of my starting them, he would ask if he could watch *Thomas the Tank Engine* or his favorite cartoon. As he began to communicate better, Lucas asked me not to show him any portion of the DVD that had been filmed in the orphanage where he had resided for the first nine months of his life. He also asked that I never speak of it. "It makes me sad," he told me.

That film from the orphanage where I had met and held Lucas for the first time is one of the happiest moments of my life. But I cannot share it with him or talk about it out of respect for his feelings.

My daughter, on the other hand, who came along two years after Lucas, would love more information on her background, but we just don't have it to give her. But this doesn't mean that she wants to celebrate her culture either.

Ever since the age of two she has expressed a strong desire to learn to speak Spanish. When she was in kindergarten, she insisted that we enroll her in a bilingual program in English and Spanish, and she has loved it and all her Spanish friends. Still, some people are surprised to find out that she doesn't study Chinese. Every time the Chinese food-delivery man appears at our door, he asks her, "You speak Chinese?" to which she responds with pride, "I speak English and Spanish!" He always shakes his head and whistles. Then he instructs her in a few basic Chinese words and their meanings. It feels as though he disapproves of me—the mother neglectful of Olivia's vital heritage.

But over the years I have continued to try. Who knows why my children won't go near the traditional Vietnamese and Chinese clothing I have bought them, not even for dress-up, which they love to play. Chances are that they would much rather pretend to be a Power Ranger or a Ninja. Stacks of adoption books gather dust on their bookshelves. When asked what his favorite part of our trip to China to get his sister was, Lucas, then four, replied, "The rides in the van!"

We have gathered with other parents who have children from Asia and have celebrated Asian culture together, presenting various homemade (or in my case store-bought) ethnic dishes. But my kids gobble up hot dogs. And though Lucas and Olivia attend racially diverse schools, not one of their friends is Asian.

I finally realized that perhaps the time had come for me to back off the cultural exposure that I so wanted my children to embrace.

It became Lucas' turn for "All about Me" week in primary school. Each day of the week a specific child was the focus of attention for a portion of the day. Lucas' teacher asked me to bring in ethnic dishes, baby photos and other items pertinent to him. I set to work and prepared a collage of baby pictures, took in a beautiful, blue silk robe that we had bought for him in Vietnam and brought in dumplings and egg rolls to make the food preparation easy on myself and palatable to the children.

Lucas sat in a circle on the floor with the rest of his class while I chatted about what a great boy he was. He basked in the glow of attention. Then, with time still left to fill before dismissal, I decided to talk about his given name and its meaning. Not just his first name, which means "dragon," but his last as well, which means that his heritage is of "royal kings" (this is what our Vietnamese adoption facilitator had told us).

Before I knew it, that little "Lord of the Flies" group took the silk robe I had brought in, shoved my son's arms into its sleeves and paraded him in a circle around the room as they shouted, "Royal king! Royal king!"

Horrified, I turned to the young teacher for direction on how to reestablish order in her classroom. But my horror turned to panic as I saw her smile down on this outrageous scene as though it were the most cherubic moment imaginable.

Lucas' head hung low in humiliation. He yelled at another boy who was pulling on his robe, "Cut it out!"

I leaned down and scooped Lucas up and away from the tiny terrors and took the robe off him. It seemed to me an eternity before the bell rang and all the children scrambled to catch their buses. Though Lucas seemed to feel much better when it was all over and didn't say anything to me about it, I wanted to drop to my knees and beg his forgiveness.

What Hurts

We all get ideas and inspiration from other parents on how to raise our children, and that can be a good thing. But I made a big mistake when, after comparing my friends Lisa's and Karen's approaches to parenting internationally adopted children, I in ignorance and self-righteousness told Lisa that if she didn't follow Karen's example and expose her son to his culture, she would be denying him his heritage.

Lisa took my comment as a criticism and a judgment of her and her husband's capabilities to parent their child, and she became angry with me. And rightly so. I believed that what I said may have cost me a friendship with her. This in turn broke my heart for my son, because Lisa's son and mine, whose birthdays are just days apart, spent the first nine months of their lives together in the same orphanage. In addition, we two couples were the only set of parents to have traveled with our adoption agency, and we experienced all the ups and downs of our journey together. Though the agency we used is based in Washington, DC, Lisa's family and mine live close to one another.

I had expected that we and our sons would remain good friends for many years to come. I thought that we had a real connection by way of shared experience and that our boys deserved to have each other in their lives. I thought that our like experience might make Lisa's son and Lucas feel a bit like brothers and that as they grew they would be able to count on each other to understand the other's feelings about being adopted.

But there I went with expectations again. I grew to realize that perhaps Lisa did not hold this comment against me. Instead, just because we shared a mostly grueling international adoption experience together, adopting young sons did not mean that a close and lasting friendship was meant to be. She and her family already had their lives, jobs, interests and relationships, and so did my husband and I. In fact, like many adoptive parents, we have drifted away from others like us as the experience of the adoptions and newness of parenting our children has faded. Not that we don't have an interest in adoption-related information or have some affiliation with adoption groups and the like, but we all move in circles that best fit our comfort levels, lifestyles, locations and needs. Oftentimes this is apart from those we initially meet on our journeys—those we feel so bonded to during such a momentous undertaking as that of flying across the globe and receiving a new child.

My comment to Lisa may have initially offended her, but more importantly, I hurt my own children as I attempted to force upon them the things of their cultures—in particular Lucas, my child who has less interest in his heritage than does his sister.

I frightened my son with dragons as a baby and caused humiliation for him in grade school by sharing his culture with his classmates. Not only this, but I set him apart from others by my focus on his Vietnamese heritage. Why had I brought in Chinese food to the class instead of the Italian dishes I know how to cook and that are so much a part of our family gatherings? Instead of an Asian silk robe and a discussion about his birth name indicating that he is the descendent of royal kings, why hadn't I talked about how his grandfather had been an Air Force pilot during World War II and had been shot down over enemy territory? And that he had survived and met Lucas' grandmother in the hospital when she as his nurse attended to him? Why had I estranged my son from family and set him up as a cultural oddity?

Grace Given

I give grace to Lisa for her anger toward me after my critical comment, although at the time I had no idea why she was so upset.

I thought my view, modeled after Karen's approach, to be best for our children and that Lisa, whose claim that her son was now Irish and that was that, had it all wrong.

But in my rush to judgment, had I forgotten how our adoption process from start to finish had been arduous and painful, with weeks spent in agony over our promised babies? Perhaps Lisa wanted to forget about Vietnam and the near nightmare we had experienced there. Maybe a celebration of all things Vietnamese and a friendship with the people with whom she had shared this terrible ordeal may have been too difficult a reminder for her of all she had been through. I cannot know.

What I do know is that I had no right to tell her how to raise her child. She was already a seasoned mother to a biological child, and I had come along as a mere neophyte in the motherhood game and told her what to do. Did I ever learn my lesson!

But I must give grace to myself too.

The lengthy process and exposure to so much of the Vietnamese people and land and culture during the wait for Lucas gave me a rich, intimate portrait of a country that is quite fascinating. After all we went through, good and bad, fond memories still linger within me, and I am grateful for all I saw and experienced. Of most importance, I came away with a stronger faith in God, which is sweet and precious to me. I simply wanted to share the good with Lucas in the hopes that he would be proud of his heritage and homeland.

We all make assumptions about various situations that touch our lives. When we experience something new and aren't sure how to process or respond to it, we often address the issue before acquiring an adequate amount of insight or information about it. I know that I have jumped to conclusions over people's offered opinions to me, and that has gotten me into trouble or offended people throughout my life more times than I can count. Other people have done it to me and will continue to do so.

All adoptive parents have unique experiences in the ways in which they do or don't expose their children to their native cultures.

For everyone with whom we have some type of relationship—and sometimes for those with whom we have only a brief encounter—there will be assumptions about what that exposure is or should be. It helps when we realize that in making such assumptions, both we and others are simply trying to make sense of things that we do not quite understand. In some circumstances people's perspectives of our parenting will come to us by way of an unsolicited opinion or a judgment. But no matter what, we need to give grace to ourselves and to others when we lack experience and understanding.

Handling It

Now, several years later, with my children the only internationally adopted kids in our large family and among their wide circle of friends, I am careful not to draw so much attention to their special heritages. I expose them to bits and pieces of their cultures here and there, and I observe how they respond. Neither of them seems too interested right now. Maybe my son's disinterest is the result of my earlier botched attempts due to my assumptions of how his life should be celebrated—although I hope not.

What I do know is that any of our expectations of how others should raise their children, whether biological or adopted, is usually not at all well received. I have also come to realize that my own expectations of how I should raise my children ought to bear this Scripture verse in mind: "Train up a child in the way he should go" (Prov. 22:6).

This verse reminds us that the most important thing to celebrate about any child is God's love for him or her. It also implies that each child is different and unique. We cannot make all our children's choices for them nor decide what their interests or passions will be. Parenting has to be tailored to the specific temperament and characteristics of each individual little one whom we are blessed to raise.

When people voice expectations or assumptions about my children's exposure to their native cultures, I don't take offense.

I remember what I have said and done and how I have hurt others like Lisa and my own precious son. I remain humbled by my own mistakes and open to Lucas and Olivia's curiosity about their backgrounds—or lack thereof.

Healing Questions

1. What has been your experience in celebrating your child's ethnic culture?

2. Have you incorporated Proverbs 22:6 into your child's life, particularly in regard to his or her cultural heritage?

3. In light of the previous two questions, what mistakes do you feel you have made in raising your child up to this point?

20

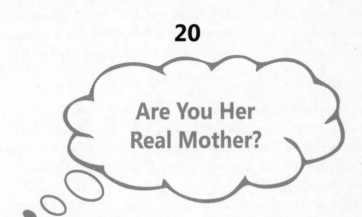

Are You Her Real Mother?

My friend and her daughter visited our home one afternoon. A sunny, summer day, my daughter and my friend's daughter jumped in and out of our pool while we mothers chatted. At some point, as Olivia stood beside me, her playdate, Amy, looked up at me and asked, "Are you Olivia's real mother?"

Though caught off guard, I knew that the six-year-old's question was innocent, filled with curiosity, and that it warranted an answer. Besides, a then-five-year-old Olivia already knew that I was not her biological mother, but no one had put that in terms of the word "real" as of yet. For both girls' sakes, I wanted to give an age-appropriate explanation.

I had just begun to answer Amy's question when Carol cut me off.

"Amy!" she cried. "We don't ask such things at a person's house."

Though I felt a bit taken aback, I told Carol, "It's OK—I want to answer her question."

"No," she said, shooting Amy a sharp look, "we'll discuss this at home."

Discuss this at home? I bristled. Who better to discuss it with her than the adoptive parent?

Carol's insistence that the matter be dropped left me deciding to acquiesce for three reasons. First of all, I did not want Amy to be scolded more. Second, I didn't want to further upset Carol. But of most importance, I didn't want Olivia to be in this awkward, uncomfortable situation in which she appeared to be at the root of it all.

What Hurts

For one thing, a reprimand toward a child for her natural and innocent curiosity can hurt that child. It can leave her feeling that to ask questions makes her guilty of doing something wrong and can stifle her normal and healthy inquisitiveness about things she wants to understand.

I know this from my own childhood and from the frustrating effect on me of not having my questions answered by the people who I thought knew everything. When these individuals gave me no response to my questions or told me not to ask, I felt shame and guilt that what I had asked was wrong or weird and therefore that there was something wrong or weird with me.

For another thing, for my friend to tell her daughter that Olivia's adoption was a topic they ought to discuss at home and not in our presence made it seem as though talking about adoption in the open was taboo. This perspective is something I fight against, because it takes this wonderful experience that each year gives thousands of children families and closets it. It turns the topic of adoption into a huge, dark cloud on a sunny afternoon—making it seem unwelcome and a threat.

My fear is that situations like the one I experienced may deliver that message to my daughter with regard to her own existence and identity—that there is something taboo about who she is.

Yes, I felt concern when Olivia observed her friend being scolded for asking if I were her real mother. She may have felt ashamed about herself and what our relationship really means, because in my daughter's five-year-old mind, no doubt Amy had done a bad thing by asking about it.

Carol did not allow me to answer a question that had been posed to me and to discuss adoption with her daughter, when, of all people, who was better to answer the question than an adoptive mother? To be frank, I felt a bit insulted when she said that she would rather talk about Olivia's adoption at home than with the very people who had experienced it. How do I know how she will handle this conversation with her child and how that may or may not coincide with what my husband and I have taught Olivia about adoption? The whole situation felt to me as if Carol was comparing adoption discussion with the airing of one's dirty laundry in public.

Grace Given

It is normal and healthy for children to be inquisitive. When they ask about things that they don't understand and receive simple, age-appropriate answers, it teaches them. Perhaps Carol has told Amy not to bring up the subject of adoption at my house, but at six years old Amy can neither be expected to remember nor to understand that this topic is, in her mother's eyes, off-limits to my daughter and me.

Maybe Olivia is Amy's only adopted friend. Amy both wants and needs to know how it is that a little Chinese girl came to be my child and what this whole adoption thing is about. At her age it is quite typical to ask questions about where babies come from, and so this information would fit into her current interest in issues such as pregnancy and birth. For instance, if Amy has been told, as many children her age are, that when a man and woman get married, God puts a baby into the mommy's tummy and then doctors take the baby out, how does adoption fit into this scenario? Wouldn't she want to know why some babies don't remain with their "real" mommies and daddies or why some children don't at all resemble their parents?

Still, although I found myself disappointed in Carol's response to Amy's question, I think Carol deserves grace.

Carol did experience firsthand my grief and my endless tears over my infertility. As part of a small group from our church that met on a weekly basis for years while I went through infertility treatments and then the adoption process, she prayed with and for me, talked with me and had great compassion for me while I suffered. Since I am the type of person who can often go overboard with both the communication and display of my emotions, Carol found herself exposed to a lot of my pain. Perhaps the fact that she scolded Amy that day may have had something to do with her attempts to protect me from the experience of any more of that awful pain.

On the flip side, Carol may have tried to shield Olivia from the question. After all, she didn't know how much my then five-year-old comprehended about her adoption or what we had discussed with her as a family. She may have thought Amy's question to be insensitive and hurtful to us both.

Handling It

As parents to internationally adopted children especially, we deserve some credit. Most of us begin discussions with our children about how they came to be part of our forever families at very early ages. We have to. Of course, I was neither offended nor unprepared for Amy's question. Things like this had already been asked of me by both my children. My husband and I have been both open and gentle with them, which is how we desire to be with their peers as well. I believe that it's so important to give children answers, to get things out in the open and then to move on. If we approach children's questions in this way, then after a few truthful answers, they often lose interest in the subject, and before we know it, they are on to the next thing in their lives such as a game of catch, a favorite snack or the latest toy on the market.

Both of my children, at approximately three or four years old, asked me, "Did I grow in your tummy?" When my son first asked this, my answer was a simple no. Unsure of just what or how much to tell him, I held off on an explanation until I knew how he would respond first. He thought about it a moment and then continued, "Well, did I grow in Daddy's tummy?"

Though I wanted to laugh, of course I didn't, and I told him once again, "No."

I have had to learn through trial and error to give young children short and simple answers to their questions and to follow their lead in sensitive conversations, because lengthy explanations are more than kids are capable of hearing and understanding. Children get overloaded with heavy content quickly. I know now that they do best with short and direct requests such as, "sit," "wait," "go," and so on. As brand-new parents, my husband and I wanted so much to help our small children learn and understand things that we often bombarded them with rambling explanations that bordered on the ridiculous. After a short time our kids' eyes would glaze over and break contact with ours, and gone would be their ability to focus on or comprehend that which we so wanted to communicate to them.

So when my son followed up his second question about growing in his daddy's tummy with, "Well, then whose tummy did I grow in?" I gave him the truth in the manner in which I thought he could receive it. Did I give him all the truth? No. I happen to know some things about his birth mother, but I realize that all the circumstances surrounding his adoption might be too painful for him to receive just yet—or maybe at all.

I told him and his sister that while God grew them in other ladies' tummies, God grew them in my heart.

Only my son has asked so far, "What other lady's tummy?" So I told him a simplistic version of the truth. I explained that she was a beautiful young woman who was unable to care for him because she did not have any money to do so. And he told me that he thought I was right, "except about the money part."

"Well, OK," I said. "But it's true." I recognize that at three or four Lucas didn't understand much about money or how it might be possible for an adult not to have any. But he left it at that and hasn't asked much about his adoption since then.

Olivia and I have had conversations about my being her real mother since that day Carol and Amy were over at our house. Every so often she reminds me that I am not her real mother, and though the pain and rejection strike me hard, I realize that hers is the heavier burden to bear. I have the joy and privilege of raising her, but she has to grapple with being given up by her birth mother. She has commented, "My own mother didn't even want me." I have swooped in on this comment with compassion and assurance that no mother ever wants to give up her baby for any reason but that sometimes things happen that force her to. Then I remind Olivia that she now has a real mother in me. To make light of a heavy situation with my young child I say, "Go ahead, touch me—I'm real." Then she starts to poke and tickle me, and she laughs.

I try to show my children each day that I am their real mother. When they are hurt, hungry, tired, upset, bored, sick or experiencing any number of difficult things, I am real, and I am there. As they grow, I tell them that although I didn't carry them in my belly, God gave them to me and me to them because their daddy and I needed babies to love and raise and because they needed parents. I also explain, in simplistic terms, that God adopts us all. I tell them that although God had but one Son, Jesus Christ, that all the rest of us can be adopted as His children too. If we ask Him, He will adopt us into His family. So adoption is meant for everyone (see Rom. 8:23). When Olivia looks up at me and asks, "Even the whole world?" I nod and say, "Yes, even the whole world."

Other children have asked questions of me and my kids about adoption. We have several young relatives in our family who have wanted to know about Lucas' and Olivia's past and heritage, among other things. I am comfortable and open with regard to their natural curiosity. This, of course, is weighed against any discomfort that my children may feel, but it is important to keep the dialogue going and the subject open so that adoption will be just a normal part of our lives.

I speak with happiness about adoption. I would love to see some of these little ones who ask questions about the matter grow up to adopt because, in part, our family may have planted a seed in them. I approach the issue from a biblical point of view and have involved my children and extended family with other adoptive families. My message is that adoption is positive and normal, because it is. It is also a privilege, an honor and a blessing, and I let my relatives know this as well.

Though we are still the only adoptive family in a fairly large extended family several years after bringing Lucas and Olivia home, I hope that someday this will change. But in this role we have both an awesome responsibility and opportunity to reflect to our family and to others the joy and fulfillment that adoption has brought to our lives. I never want to sweep the subject under the rug as though it doesn't exist, because adoption is our beautiful, God-orchestrated reality. It's my testimony about a life that was once filled with lack and sorrow but has now been transformed. God has now made me a "childless woman in her home as a happy mother of children" (Ps. 113:9 NIV). Who wouldn't want to share that? And as a Christian, I am obliged to share that.

Healing Questions

1. Has anyone ever asked you if you are your child's real parent? If not, what adverse things might someone have said to you about your relationship with your adopted child?

2. How did you or would you respond to such a question?

3. How important is it to you to either share details about your adoption with others or to keep things private? Why?

21

Just Like One of the Family

While at a writer's conference one spring in New York City, I presented some of my writing material on adoption to the members of a class that I was taking. This prompted another adoptive mother to approach me after the class and to talk with me about her now middle-aged adopted child.

As we chatted, I could tell that she loved her son a great deal. But what surprised me was what she said of another adopted child in her extended family. As she told me of other relatives who had followed in her footsteps to bring nonbiological children into their lives and homes, she described one particular child and said, "She's just like one of the family."

I must say, as another adoptive parent, that I felt a little taken aback, and my initial thought was that this woman ought to know better than to say something like that. I wondered why she did not recognize, since she had an adopted child of her own, that her statement sounded like a bit of a slight toward adopted children.

This wasn't the first time I had heard the statement, although it happened to be the only time another adoptive parent had said it to me. It raised a red flag for me, since adoption should include a complete and total acceptance of any adopted child as family.

What Hurts

With two simple words, "just" and "like," an adopted child is made similar to but not the same as family. These words communicate an inference that genetics produces family, but adoption creates something else like it.

Over the years my own large family has incorporated dear friends into our lives in many ways. We've often said of them, "They're like one of the family." We know that they and we are not blood related, but we care for them a great deal and want their participation in our lives at parties and gatherings and important events. But we don't share highly personal family information with them, nor do we name them as our relatives, because, of course, they are not. We don't share surnames with them, send their kids to school, pay for their expenses or house them. They're friends, after all, not family.

But a child whom God blesses us with who does not share in our DNA nonetheless becomes one of us. Adopted children are not like us, rather they are one with us. We teach them about their family tree, which for us includes ancestors who have emigrated from Europe. They have our last name, share our home and are entitled to our estate. They even share in some of our mannerisms, likes and, quite possibly, quirks.

Imitations are often a lot like the real thing. Bootleg items sold on the streets, a "Rolex" watch that you can buy from a vendor for twenty bucks, knockoffs of famous brands and "me too" products—those that flood the marketplace and are meant to cater to a need but aren't quite the original—this is the stuff of "like."

But things that are like the real thing are always off and inferior in some way. We bring them into our homes and realize that they are damaged or flawed. I do not like the connotations of such a phrase as "just like" associated with my family.

Grace Given

During my conversation with this fellow conference attendee, I saw before me a lovely older woman who I believe loved the Lord. After all, we happened to be at a Christian conference. Though I certainly could not know her heart from a ten-minute chat, the woman came across as personable, friendly and content. She clearly loved her children and her extended family. I don't believe for a minute that she meant any harm or slight to anyone.

In fact, people often use this "just like" phrase in speaking well of their adopted friends and family. They often say it with a smile, and the inference is that they approve of the adopted parents' decision to take in an abandoned child. They have genuine love and concern for the adopted member of the family and feel that things have worked out well for everyone involved.

Handling It

I do feel the urge to tell people who use the "just like" phrase that the adopted person is part of the family. But on that particular spring afternoon, as I sat at a desk and looked up at this other adoptive parent, I refrained from correcting her. Maybe it was the way her eyes lit up when she spoke of these relatives of hers that prevented me from doing so. Or perhaps it was the realization that she had adopted a half century ago and that her way of referring to her adopted family was part of the lingo people used way back then. It could have been that all those years of my parents telling me to respect my elders restrained me from telling this lovely, elderly woman how she should speak of her family. The Holy Spirit may have even prompted me to keep my tongue. I simply do not know.

I do know that what may seem an opportunity to correct another or to reproach them is not always an opportunity at all and therefore should not necessarily be seized upon.

God's Word tells us to "be quick to hear" and "slow to speak" (James 1:19). We often need wisdom to understand another's frame of reference and gentleness when we address what we think others misunderstand. I realize that I am a work in progress with regard to these characteristics, and I want to be sensitive to others. Of course, there is often conflict between my mouth, which rushes to speak, and the mouth that is instructed by God to be slow to speak.

Many Christians I have encountered struggle with discernment when it comes to either grabbing hold of a perceived moment of opportunity or holding back until an opportune time. I saw this happen often when I got acquainted with the church in New York City in which I first began to learn about the Lord.

Teams of young Christians from this church would jump on subway cars and evangelize to the strangers around them. I had been instructed, even though I had not yet accepted Christ, to do the same. But it terrified me to approach people I did not know in that way. So I tried it instead with some of the regular patrons who sat and drank at the bar of a restaurant where I worked. But my "good news" became their fodder for the most awful, crude and irreverent jokes I had ever heard. You see, I had "cast [my] pearls before swine" (Matt. 7:6, KJV). Simply put, I gave words of wisdom to those who would not listen or appreciate what I had to say.

Often the young Christians who meant to mentor me as I struggled with a grasp of God's Word and with how to surrender my life to Him spoke unwisely as well. They assessed my slow progress with quick reproaches such as, "You just don't love God enough," or, "I feel sorry for you."

Rather than trying to understand my past, my skewed notions about God or the real issues that I needed help with, the only attempt my church made to get to know my heart was to demand that I create a comprehensive list of every sin I had ever committed and present it to someone who was a virtual stranger to me. With my teary-eyed, ashamed refusal came the verdict that I was no longer eligible for salvation.

It's not a surprise that I did not become saved at this church. It was later on, after receiving some good pastoral counsel and the insight that God loved me, not my evangelism skills or my thick-skulled efforts to do right, that I received the Lord.

Through these types of experiences, I have learned that legalistic churches like the one I encountered are sometimes in such a rush to do the Lord's work and to bring people to Christ and to make great disciples who can in turn disciple others that they sometimes consider every door an open one through which they should burst.

But just as in the case of taking a leap forward to save a soul and to share God's Word, so a rush to change a person's perception about any topic can do more harm than good.

How can one save a soul but reject a heart? How can one change a heart or a false assumption without first implementing grace and understanding?

It is God's kindness that leads us to repentance (see Rom. 2:4). That is why it is important for us to deal with a perceived injustice or offense with grace. We must give others the benefit of the doubt, as God surely led me to do with the woman who spoke of her adopted relative as "just like" one of the family.

But whether we are to speak or to remain silent in a given situation, it is vital that we who are adoptive parents understand what God has to say about the matter.

God's Word paints a beautiful picture of adoption.

Ephesians 1:5 says, "he predestined us for adoption as sons through Jesus Christ, according to the purpose of his will." And in Galatians 4:4–7 we read, "God sent forth his Son, born of woman . . . so that we might receive adoption as sons. And because you are sons, God has sent the Spirit of his Son into our hearts . . . So you are no longer a slave, but a son, and if a son, then an heir through God."

I tell my children that adoption is God's plan for all of us. I further tell them that in Acts 17:26–27 the Word says, "And he made from one man every nation of mankind . . . having determined allotted periods and the boundaries of their dwelling place, that they should seek God, and perhaps feel their way toward him and find him. Yet he is actually not far from each one of us."

When I share these truths with my kids, I hope to communicate to their impressionable minds that adoption is not only for them but for all humankind. Adoption does not make them different in God's eyes, because we all eagerly await our adoptions (see Rom. 8:23). My children's adoptions and their lives with their father and me are circumstances that God created so that my kids could learn about Him and love Him, because they are dearly loved by Him. I know that had Lucas been raised in Vietnam and Olivia in China, they might not have been taught about Christ. Or worse, it may have been ingrained in them to reject Him.

My children need to know that adoption is something that God plans for us all and that through His love and wisdom, He chose when each of us would be born and where we would live. This, I pray, will foster in them a sense of not only awe and thanks to God but also of confidence and security in the One who gave them their lives and their family. This is of vital importance to adoptive children who may grow up to question why they were given up, whether they were loved by a birth parent or what their lives might have been like had they remained with biological families.

As believers in Christ who await our official adoptions, don't we often have to leave family behind too? Don't we sometimes lose connections with family members who don't share our love of the Lord and our desire to please Him? Don't they sometimes abandon us as well?

As we grow in relationship with Christ, we incorporate His traits into our own expressions and behaviors toward others. Just as a child models his or her parent, so Christians too reflect the character and nature of Christ. We all share the same heavenly Father, and we say of one another, "He is my brother in Christ," or, "She is my sister in the Lord." We never say, "They are like my brothers and sisters in Jesus Christ," or, "We are like the body of Christ." Each of us belongs, we are all united with one another, and we all share in the same inheritance. My children are my family.

Healing Questions

1. After having read this book, what are your thoughts on giving grace and on trying to understand people who say hurtful words?

2. How will you incorporate what the Bible has to say about adoption with what you tell your children about it?

3. How has this book helped you to forgive those who have said things that have hurt you?

Appendix of Recommended Resources

Two Christian-based support groups for those who have suffered or are suffering through the heartache of infertility and/or loss are Hannah's Prayer Ministries (www.hannah.org) and Parenting After Infertility and Loss Ministries (www.parentingafterinfertility.com).

Another good source of support for couples dealing with infertility is Stepping Stones at step.bethany.org.

My own website, www.christinerhyner.com, is designed for women who adopt after infertility. My blog contains a wide range of topics on these issues.

To understand more about reproductive technologies, visit the Center for Bioethics & Human Dignity at www.cbhd.org. There you will find information and analysis on all the latest medical technology from a Christian perspective.

Og Mandino, in his book *The Greatest Mystery in the World*, provides an insightful look at life from the moment of conception. Though not a book about reproductive technologies or fertility treatments, it is a godly source for driving home the ramifications of issues such as embryo freezing.

The following books provide some good reading on spiritual warfare: *Battlefield of the Mind: Winning the Battle in Your Mind* by Joyce Meyer, *The Bondage Breaker: Overcoming Negative Thoughts, Irrational Feelings, Habitual Sins* by Neil T. Anderson and *Victory in Spiritual Warfare: Outfitting Yourself for the Battle* by Tony Evans.

Notes

Chapter 1

1. Joyce Meyer, *Living Beyond Your Feelings: Controlling Emotions—So They Don't Control You* (New York: FaithWords, 2011), 215.

Chapter 4

1. "Myths and Facts About Infertility," RESOLVE, http://www.resolve.org/support-and-services/for-family--friends/myths-and-facts.html, (accessed October 14, 2013).

2. Danielle Pennel, "Adopting Does Not Improve Your Fertility," *My Paperwork Pregnancies* on Adoptive Families Circle, April 2010, http://www.adoptivefamiliescircle.com/blogs/post/adopting_does_not_improve_your_fertility/ (accessed December 2013).

Chapter 6

1. Matt Rosenberg, "China's One Child Policy: One Child Policy in China Designed to Limit Population Growth," About.com, August 12, 2012 http://geography.about.com/od/populationgeography/a/onechild.htm (accessed August 20, 2013).

Chapter 14

1. Definition of "astrology," *Webster's New World Dictionary and Thesaurus* (New York: Simon & Schuster, 1996), 35.

2. Amber McKynzie, "You Don't Say! 10 Unbelievable Myths About Black People," Black Enterprise, March 27, 2013, http://www.blackenterprise.com/functional/black-history-month/10-black-people-myths-stereotypes-unbelieveable/ (accessed December 2013).

Chapter 15

1. "Ching chong," Wikipedia, https://en.wikipedia.org/wiki/Ching_chong (accessed December 2013).

2. Ibid.

Chapter 16

1. "An Open Letter from the Asian American Community to the Evangelical Church," Next Gener.Asian Church, October 13, 2013, http://nextgenerasianchurch.com/2013/10/13/an-open-letter-to-the-evangelical-church-from-the-asian-american-community/ (accessed December 2013).

2. Karen Grigsby Bates, "Asian-Americans To Evangelicals: We're Not Your Punch Line," Code Switch for National Public Radio, October 18, 2013, http://www.npr.org/blogs/codeswitch/2013/10/17/236380656/asian-americans-to-evangelicals-were-not-your-punchline (accessed December 2013).

3. Ibid.

4. Ibid.

5. "Open Letter from the Asian American Community."

6. Definition of "ignorant," *The American Heritage Dictionary of the English Language,* online, http://www.ahdictionary.com/word/search.html?q=ignorant (accessed December 2013).

PUBLICATIONS

Fort Washington, PA 19034

This book is published by CLC Publications, an outreach of CLC Ministries International. The purpose of CLC is to make evangelical Christian literature available to all nations so that people may come to faith and maturity in the Lord Jesus Christ. We hope this book has been life changing and has enriched your walk with God through the work of the Holy Spirit. If you would like to know more about CLC, we invite you to visit our website:

www.clcusa.org

To know more about the remarkable story of the founding of CLC International we encourage you to read

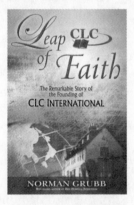

LEAP OF FAITH

Norman Grubb

Paperback
Size 5¹/₄ x 8, Pages 249
ISBN: 978-0-87508-650-7 - $11.99
ISBN (*e-book*): 978-1-61958-055-8 - $9.99

RESISTING GOSSIP

Matthew C. Mitchell

With gossip being so prevalent in our culture, it can be hard to resist listening to and sharing stories about other people's business. But what does God say about gossip? In *Resisting Gossip*, Pastor Matt Mitchell not only outlines the scriptural warnings against gossip, but also demonstrates how the truth of the gospel can deliver believers from this temptation.

Paperback
Size 5¼ x 8, Pages 182
ISBN: 978-1-61958-076-3 - $13.99
ISBN (*e-book*): 978-1-61958-077-0 - $9.99

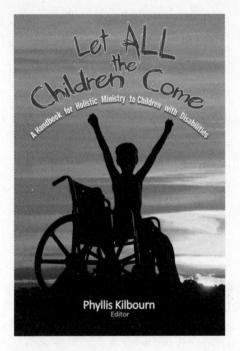

LET ALL THE CHILDREN COME

Phyllis Kilbourn

In order to minister more effectively to children with
disabilities, we first must understand the context surrounding
children with disabilities and the consequences of disability
on them. This book, compiled by Phyllis Kilbourn, provides
helpful training to those who desire to engage in more informed
ministry to disabled children.

Paperback
Size 6 x 9, Pages 414
ISBN: 978-1-61958-067-1 - $14.99
ISBN (*e-book*): 978-1-61958-128-9 - $9.99

eSHIFT

David A. Posthuma

eShift: The Decline of "Attractional" Church and the Rise of the Internet-Influenced Church teaches readers how to distinguish between the established culture and the present-emerging culture as it relates to the church. This dynamic book shows how this vast culture-gap can be bridged for the sake of Christ's mission in the world.

Paperback
Size 5¹/₄ x 8, Pages 208
ISBN: 978-1-61958-086-2 - $13.99
ISBN (*e-book*): 978-1-61958-087-9 - $9.99

TOO AMAZING TO KEEP TO YOURSELF

Ken Wilson

A great tool for both individuals and small groups, *Too Amazing to Keep to Yourself* is an interactive guidebook that will equip you with the message, skills and passion to bring people to Christ in a way that is safe and nonthreatening for both you and your friends.

Paperback
Size 6 x 9, Pages 207
ISBN: 978-1-61958-154-8 - $14.99
ISBN (*e-book*): 978-1-61958-155-5 - $9.99

HEALING FOR HURTING HEARTS

Phyllis Kilbourn

With its practical and biblically-centered instruction on counseling children and youth in crisis, *Healing for Hurting Hearts* equips leaders to guide the children they serve through the healing process in order to help them achieve lives that are more abundant.

Paperback
Size 6 x 9, Pages 302
ISBN: 978-1-61958-084-8 - $14.99
ISBN (*e-book*): 978-1-61958-085-5 - $9.99

RUNNING ON EMPTY

Jill Briscoe

Feeling burned out? Unfulfilled? Drained? Jill Briscoe offers hope and comfort for those times in life when we feel empty and tired. With wit and candor, Briscoe draws lessons from several biblical figures that provide spiritual refreshment and renewal to those who are *Running on Empty*.

Paperback
Size 5¹/₄ x 8, Pages 176
ISBN: 978-1-61958-080-0 - $12.99
ISBN (*e-book*): 978-1-61958-081-7 - $9.99

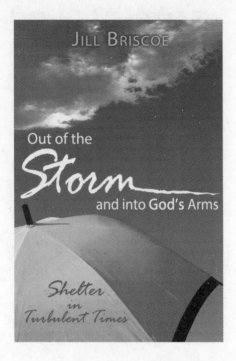

OUT OF THE STORM

Jill Briscoe

What do you do when the storm clouds of life surround you—and you can't see the silver lining? Where do you turn when God feels distant? Exploring truths from the book of Job, Jill Briscoe addresses the tough issues involved in the collision of affliction and faith.

Paperback
Size 5¹/₄ x 8, Pages 208
ISBN: 978-1-61958-008-4 - $12.99
ISBN (*e-book*): 978-1-61958-021-3 - $9.99

GETTING INTO GOD

Stuart Briscoe

Stuart Briscoe's *Getting into God* will take you through the basic elements of biblical study, prayer and witnessing. Whether you are a new Christian or one simply wanting to get back to the basics of your faith, this book offers some basic instruction on the "practicalities of Christian experience."

Paperback
Size 5¹/₄ x 8, Pages 144
ISBN: 978-1-61958-152-4 - $11.99
ISBN (*e-book*): 978-1-61958-153-1 - $9.99